JACK WEISS

MEMORIES
DREAMS
NIGHTMARES

MEMOIRS OF A HOLOCAUST SURVIVOR

UNIVERSITY OF
CALGARY
PRESS

© 2005 JACK WEISS

Published by the University of Calgary Press
2500 University Drive NW, Calgary, Alberta, Canada T2N 1N4
www.uofcpress.com

LIBRARY AND ARCHIVES CANADA CATALOGUING IN PUBLICATION

Weiss, Jack, 1930-
    Memories, dreams, nightmares : memoirs of a holocaust
survivor / Jack Weiss.

(Legacies shared, ISSN 1498-2358 ; 13)
Includes index.
ISBN 1-55238-126-9

    1. Weiss, Jack, 1930- 2. Jews—Hungary—Biography. 3. Holocaust,
Jewish (1939-1945)—Personal narratives. 4. Holocaust survivors—
Canada—Biography. I. Title. II. Series.

DS135.H93W46 2004   940.53'18'092   C2004-906585-8

We acknowledge the financial support of the Government of Canada
through the Book Publishing Industry Development Program (BPIDP) and
the Alberta Foundation for the Arts. We acknowledge the support of the
Canada Council for the Arts for our publishing program.

Printed and bound in Canada by Kromar Printing Ltd.
♾ This book is printed on 70 lb. Accent Opaque
Cover design, page design and typesetting by Mieka West

Canada Council   Conseil des Arts
for the Arts   du Canada

In loving memory of my late brother-in-law Gerald Potasky, whose heartfelt compassion toward, and interest in, my original manuscript encouraged me and fuelled my desire to complete my autobiography.

I was very fortunate in being able to come to Canada, the best country in the world. I prayed to God that I would one day have a normal life, to be loved and accepted. I met the most wonderful girl – my wife. She was always at my side, encouraging me, loving me and helping me, even though I wasn't always the easiest person to live with. Her parents, brother and sister accepted and loved me and treated me as one of the family. This encouraged me and made me strive to better myself, to be a good husband, father, grandfather and a good citizen of Canada. I hope I reached my goal.

Jack and Sara, 2002

PREFACE

I am still here, alive and relatively well. In this day and age, and at the age of 73, this is not considered much of an achievement, but in my case it is a miracle. Why do some people perish by freak accident in a safe environment, or from disease in a medically superior society, while others like myself survive the atrocities of war, when the goal of a nation is to exterminate us? I did not survive unscathed. My experience robbed me of my trust in humanity and my ever having a feeling of security. Pre-war and times of war have scarred me for life.

Yet … I have my blessings.…

My sons realized at a very early age that I did not have parents, sisters, brothers, or any family, and that I spoke with an accent. They were curious and started asking questions.

I felt it was my moral obligation to tell my children about my parents, my sisters and brother, my unhappy childhood, and the horrors of the Holocaust. This is what prompted me to write my autobiography. I wanted it to be a memorial for my family, and I wanted the story of the Holocaust to be told to future generations, never to be forgotten, never to happen again.

I have been very fortunate having a devoted wife, and we were blessed with two sons, Stephen Joel (Steve) and Jerome Sheldon (Jerry). They are both dentists and have a successful dental practice. Steve is married to Cheryl (nee Shore). They have four children, a son, Macey Lee, and three daughters, Mallory Barbra, Lauren Nicole, and Marlee Dana. Jerry is married to Audrey (nee Shaffer). They have two children, Jenna Gabrielle and Joshua Philip. They are beautiful, bright children. We are very proud of our family and love them dearly.

My wife, children, and grandchildren have been a source of pride and joy to me and I have been blessed with their sincere and limitless love.

I dedicate this book to my wife, children, and grandchildren.

Edited by Karen (Joseph) Dennis, with my sincere thanks. My sincere thanks to Jamis Paulson, Communications, Programming and Outreach Director, Manitoba Writers Guild Inc. for his patience and assistance.

I have a problem: my grandchildren don't like my accent. Yesterday I was teaching them how to blow their noses, now they're teaching me how to speak

English. Lauren, my son Stephen's daughter, corrects my pronunciation.

Not mudder, Zaida, mo-ther.

Zaida comes from Europe, her father explains. He was born in Hungary then moved to Czechoslovakia.

No, Stephen, you've got it wrong. I was born in Czechoslovakia. Later, it became Hungary.

How can I expect my son to understand? He was born and raised in Canada, whose borders haven't changed in a hundred years. I went to sleep in one country and woke up in another. My sons, both college graduates, only speak one of Canada's two "official" languages; their father, a Grade five dropout, had to make himself understood in Czech, Hungarian, Ukrainian, Yiddish, Polish, and German just to survive into his teens – at which point he picked up Hebrew and Italian. I never knew from day to day what language I would speak, what flag I would salute, where I would lay my head at night, or where my next crust of bread was coming from. It was a world of chaos from which, by some miracle, I managed to escape and to which I have never returned.

Except in my dreams.

Today I'm called Jack Weiss, but I was born Erno Weisz – or *Weisz Erno* as they say in Central Europe. A German Camp functionary said Erno wasn't a "real" name and gave me a new name: *Ernst*. After the liberation I joined a kibbutz and became *Yakov*, which is my Hebrew name. What's in a name? Everyone calls my wife *Sue* but her parents named her *Sara*. Sarah, the wife of the Patriarch Abraham, is the "Mother" of the Jewish people. She is considered a saint.

My Suzy is also a saint. She's been married to me for fifty years. I am not an easy person to live with. I'm impatient, short-tempered, and moody. I don't sleep well. I have nightmares.

You would think I'd be over them by now. When I came to Canada, at the age of seventeen, I had my whole life ahead of me. And it's been a good life. In the past half-century, I've never gone hungry or been without gainful employment. I've worked in the fur trade, owned a few businesses – some successful, some not – was a transit driver for a number of years, and now I'm retired on a pension. I turned seventy with the new millennium but still have my hearing, my eyesight, most of my hair – which is just tinged with grey – and am fit enough to play golf with friends a few times a week. I have everything a man my age could ask for: a beautiful, intelligent wife, two successful and happily married sons, and six wonderful grandchildren, whom I love dearly.

And I have nightmares.

Someone told me the bad dreams might go away if I wrote about my experiences, but I've never been able to do it. Some things are too disturbing to think about, never mind dwell on. When I came to Canada in 1948, I wanted to forget my miserable childhood, not relive it, but I want my sons to know where they came from. I want my grandchildren to understand why *Zaida* doesn't talk like the rest of the family. And time is running out. Not only for me, but for all my fellow survivors. If those who know the truth remain silent, the truth will be lost. There will be no eyewitnesses left to contradict the "historians" who now deny that the greatest crime in the history of humanity ever took place. There will be only well-meaning movie moguls to give us the Hollywood version.

When Steven Spielberg decided to make a movie about the Holocaust, all the financial experts said he was committing career suicide. They were wrong. It's a wonderful thing that a big Hollywood producer would take such a risk. Without movies like *Schindler's List* to remind them, most people would forget who Hitler was and what he did.

I didn't go to see Mr. Spielberg's Academy Award-winning movie.

I don't have to be reminded.

I have nightmares....

INTRODUCTION

Near the end of his memoir, Jack Weiss makes a statement that crystallizes the fact that each person who lived through the Holocaust lived through a different Holocaust. In Weiss's case, he describes his childhood as miserable, his early adolescence made additionally bleak by the early stages of the war, his period in the camps shorter than that of many others but ending dramatically with the Death March westward Nazi officers forced inmates of the eastern camps to make in retreat before the advancing Russians. It is one of the ironies of his tale that a fellow inmate of Auschwitz-Birkenau, a shoemaker from Weiss's own town of Beregszasz too sick to evacuate and certain that his death will be caused by the threatened torching of all buildings by the Nazis, instead makes it home before Weiss does.

Jack Weiss (his final, Canadian, name) indeed has an eye for irony. Self-described as immature and underdeveloped, he is only fourteen when Hungary finally gives in to German pressure to round up its Jews. Desperate to stay with his forty-four-year-old father, the child puffs himself up as a man, passing

inspection on arrival at Auschwitz by a man he re-
members as Joseph Mengele and fleeing from soldiers
charged with capturing – for termination – boys too
young to work. The moment he is given his tattoo,
then, is a welcome one.

> You don't brand an animal you are going to slaughter.
> Years later my tattoo would become a painful remind-
> er, but at the time it was a great relief. I was perfectly
> happy to trade my identity as Weisz, Erno, gas cham-
> ber candidate, for Weisz, Ernst, slave labourer A-9654.
> My father was A-9655.

Weiss's relationship with that father is another irony.
A Jew so secular that his wife's family called him Goy,
Solomon Weisz was a successful hard-working baker
in 1930 when his son was born. When his wife died
in 1934, he allowed his daughter to be adopted but
kept his son, who fairly soon would become half-
brother to two more sisters and a brother. Already
financially strained by his first wife's medical bills,
Solomon eventually lost the bakery and was forced to
spend more and more time away, mixing his dough
at home, baking his bagels on charity at the bakery
that once was his and travelling to country fairs.
Heartbreakingly, Weiss states that "I worshiped my

father, but he displayed no feeling for me whatsoever." Before the internment of father and son in the late spring of 1944, Weiss is at the mercy of his frustrated stepmother, experiences growing anti-semitism, is evacuated across the Dnieper, and escapes to live alternately with his father and his mother's family. Always, Weiss tries to get back to a father who does little to protect him but whom he will protect at Auschwitz as long as he can.

Weiss insists that not only was his life miserable, he himself was a "bum." Certainly, the grudging acceptance given him by his mother's family would do little to bolster his self-confidence. A much fonder memory is a short heavenly holiday with his father's converted half-brother in Budapest. Still, the sense of responsibility family members show for one another provides added insight into the profundity of the horror that was the Holocaust. Weiss is not alone in seeking out years later friends and family and old acquaintances.

Neither is Weiss alone in claiming to have written a memoir as "a memorial for my family." What is unusual – and refreshing – is his self-characterization as "bum." Habits formed for self-protection in childhood helped him and his father in Auschwitz and may account for his survival on the Death March, but they made him not always malleable to those charged with sorting out the chaos that followed the Final Solution. Recruited to go to Israel at such time as the embargo should lift, Weiss kicked around Austria and Italy, rebelliously self-sufficient when at all possible. His coming to Canada, to Winnipeg, was almost a fluke.

As it turned out, it was a lucky one. Always a hard worker and now in a place where he could legitimately build a home, Weiss married, fathered two sons, worked and owned businesses – and explained to his grandchildren why he spoke English differently than they did and seemed to have no relatives. A trip to Israel reunites him with old friends he thought lost to him. He knows his father is dead and assumes the same of his stepmother, stepsisters and stepbrother. His memoirs end with the results of his search for the sister he had seen only once after their mother's death.

Throughout this life, Jack Weiss has nursed memories, dreamt dreams, and woken in terror from nightmares. In his seventies, he sifted through them for his family. He has also decided to share them with us.

Janice Dickin
University of Calgary

PART ONE
EUROPE
(1930–47)

EARLY YEARS

Whenever people discuss the Holocaust, one question always arises. Why did the Jews allow themselves to be slaughtered? Why didn't they rise up in arms against their oppressors rather than meekly cooperate in their own destruction? The answer is that the Jews of Europe had no idea what lay in store for them until it was too late. The Nazis did not advertise the "Final Solution." Their method was to lull their victims with lies, to cultivate false hope, to convince the Jews of Europe that things couldn't possibly be that bad. Pressures built up so gradually that, at first, they did not seem more than mildly threatening. The Holocaust was entirely outside of everyone's experience. The Jewish people had survived five thousand years of bloody persecution and we would survive this. I was too young to know what was going on, but my father suffered each new blow to his freedom, his pride, and his humanity, always hoping it would be the last. *Weisz Solomon* had no way of knowing that history wasn't simply repeating itself, that there *was* something new under the Sun.

In 1930, the year I was born, my father had a successful bakery business in Bereghovo, a picturesque city at the foot of the Carpathian Mountains, just west of the Ukraine. Before the formation of Czechoslovakia in 1914, at the end of the First World War, Bereghovo had been part of the Austro-Hungarian Empire, and the prevailing language and sentiment were still Hungarian. Over the teacher's desk in school hung a picture of Miklos Horthy, the Regent of Hungary, and every morning we sang not the Czechoslovakian national anthem but a Hungarian song about how we were living in a "broken land" that would someday be united with Mother Hungary.

My father had no such longing for a united Hungary. He was proud to be a citizen of Czechoslovakia, the most enlightened nation in Europe. It wasn't his country that was broken, but his family. He had heard about a half-brother living in Budapest, whom he had never met, but the rest of the family was dispersed to the four winds. A tall, thin man with a black moustache and short military haircut, Solomon Weisz was a secular Jew who only went to the synagogue on the High Holidays for the sake of appearances (the owner of a kosher bakery couldn't afford to alienate his customers) and rarely spoke Yiddish, preferring Czech or Hungarian.

In this respect, he was no different from most of the others in our hometown. The only Jews in Bereghovo who spoke Yiddish as a first language were those who came from Eastern Europe, as my stepmother did. Bereghovo was not Warsaw – there was a Jewish quarter, where my father's bakery was located, but nothing even close to a ghetto. The Jews of Central Europe were completely integrated into the community. Even the men on my mother's side of the family, who were highly religious, didn't wear long beards and fur hats but looked and dressed much like the other prosperous farmers in the area.

My mother's family had no use for my father. They called him a *Goy* (Gentile). He, for his part, considered them pious hypocrites. My father didn't lie, cheat, or steal from his customers – that was *his* religion. Though he was a businessman, his political philosophy was closer to Communism than capitalism. But I know he believed in God because he would talk to Him. When it rained on a market day, for instance, he would look at the sky and say, "You had to do it to me, didn't you? Six dozen bagels down the drain!"

Solomon Weisz did not observe the laws of Orthodox Judaism, but when unforeseeable disasters rained down on his life he would revert to the practice of his forefathers and complain to God. As time went on, he had more and more to complain about.

And so did his son.

I worshiped my father, but he displayed no feeling for me whatsoever. He was not a demonstrative person. The only time he spoke to me was to scold or criticize. "You should have more *chaine*," he would tell me constantly. *Chaine* is a Yiddish word for which there is no English equivalent. "Charm" is close but not the same. For example, some children will spontaneously give you a hug and kiss – they have *chaine*. Other children will sit in a corner and hope you don't notice them – that was me.

Maybe the first few years of my life were happy – I don't remember. At the age of fourteen, I was loaded onto a boxcar and shipped to Auschwitz, but my personal holocaust began the day my mother died. She loved me dearly, but because she had a chronic kidney problem and wasn't able to care for her two young children, my father's unmarried half-sister became a surrogate mother to me and my baby sister, Szidi. I can still clearly picture *Yolanka Nainie* (Aunt Yolanka), but the only memory I have of my mother is of a nice lady who was always in bed. The only photograph I have shows a pleasant-looking woman with a square face, straight nose, and kind eyes who bears a striking resemblance to me.

I inherited my mother's looks and my father's personality. He was a stubbornly independent man who never did anything halfway. He worked like a horse, ate like a horse (without gaining weight), and smoked like a chimney. A baker's life is not an easy life. You go to work in the middle of the night, come home in the middle of the day, catch a few hours of sleep, have a bite to eat, then go back to the bakery. And with a sick wife to add to his burden, my father did not have a great deal of time or patience for his children.

Although my father had no real feeling for me as an individual, he took pride in having produced a son who he hoped was a younger version of himself. On Sundays, the only day his bakery was closed, he would take me for a walk around the neighbourhood to show me off to his friends and customers. "This is my son," he would say, as if the little man in a Czechoslovakian army uniform could be anyone else's.

As a young man, my father had been a bit of a vagabond. He had tried his hand at a number of jobs – including circus clown – but the highlight of his early career was the time he spent as an army cook. "An army travels on its stomach," Napoleon said. In the military a good cook is treated with more respect than a general, and my father – who would prepare special dishes for his commanding officer – was a very good cook. The years he spent in the Czechoslovakian army were the happiest years of his life. He was so proud of his service that, years later, he had a smaller version of his uniform made for his three-year-old son.

I don't remember parading around town in my fancy uniform, but I've seen a photograph of myself wearing it, and it must have cost a fortune. It was accurate in every detail, right down to the little sword dragging on the ground behind me. Unfortunately, due to some bad acting on my part, the show closed before I outgrew my costume.

One wet spring day, on our Sunday walk, I saw a toy in a store window and I asked my father to buy it. He tried to explain that the store was closed, but I didn't understand. All I knew was that I wanted the toy and he wouldn't buy it for me. I also knew that he loved to show me off in my little uniform so, to punish him, I sat down in a mud puddle.

My father never took me for a walk again. (Years later, Yolanka Nainie, who told me the story, said the day after the mud puddle incident she saw my uniform in the trash bin by the front door.)

Apparently my father was not prepared to put up with my *shtick,* so it must have been my mother who spoiled me rotten. I don't know how they got together since they were so different. It certainly wasn't an arranged marriage. My father was a secular Jew with virtually no family ties; my mother was the youngest daughter of a large family of ultra-Orthodox Jewish landholders who had lived in the area for centuries.

As a child, I had virtually no contact with my mother's side of the family. The Blaus had no use for my father, and the feeling was mutual. When I was forced to live with my maternal uncles for a few days as a young man, they treated me like dirt. My mother's family came from a tiny *shtetl* called Tarpa, about thirty kilometres from Bereghovo, on the Hungarian side of the border. Her father was a watchmaker and her mother gave birth to nine children (six girls and three boys) of whom my mother was the youngest. A young woman from a well-to-do family didn't have to marry the first *schlemiel* who came along, so Zali Blau must have seen *something* in the tall, dark, but not particularly handsome nonbeliever.

My father may not have been Prince Charming, but he was a good provider. Whatever he did, he did well. People would come from miles around to buy the *ayer kichlach* (egg bagels) he made that would melt in your mouth. By the time I was born, my father had a thriving business and for the first four years of my

My mother

life we lived in a modern apartment in a nice part of town. But hard times were just around the corner. My father's business was going downhill even before the government took it away. My mother's illness drained his resources as well as his spirit. He couldn't look after a thriving bakery, a sick wife, and two infant children so Yolanka Nainie nursed my mother and took over the household. She was a fine person who cared a great deal for my little sister and me, but she couldn't work miracles. The doctor's bills kept piling up and my mother kept getting sicker. Then one day while I was playing on the floor in my mother's room, she asked me to come and lie down beside her. I can remember this incident vividly.

"I don't want to."

"Please, just for a minute."

So I climb onto the bed beside her.

She hugs me and starts to cry.

"My poor child, what's going to happen when I die?"

I think she is really asking me a question.

"When people die, they bury them."

That was my answer and it haunts me still. A short time later, on the first day of Passover, 1934, my answer came to pass.

I had just celebrated my fourth birthday.

My *happy* childhood was over.

Stepchild

If Yolanka Nainie expected my father to marry her – they weren't related by blood – she was in for a disappointment. She did eventually marry and have a child, and in later years, whenever she met me on the street, she was very loving and concerned, and she always invited me to her place for a meal. Meanwhile, my father had found a younger and more attractive candidate.

Lenka Simcovitch was a pretty blond woman in her early twenties who came from a tiny village near the Ukrainian border. My father wasn't exactly a young Valentino but to an unsophisticated girl from a poor family, an older man with an established business must have seemed like quite a catch.. True, she had to take his spoiled son into the bargain but nothing in life is perfect. At least my father had gotten rid of his other brat.

After my mother died, my sister, Szidi, was given up for adoption to a childless Jewish couple who lived in Fehkete Ardo, a small town about 45 kilometres from Bereghovo. One of my maternal uncles offered to adopt me (a farm can always use another hand), but my father wasn't interested in having his only son brought up as "a proper Jew." He would rather find me a new mother.

My stepmother was a tough cookie. She was a small woman, but she terrified me.. She had a will of iron and a bad temper. If I didn't do exactly what I was told, when I was told, I would get a slap. She even managed to turn my father against me. The second he walked in the door, exhausted from working all day and half the night, she would start to complain. I was bad, I wouldn't do what I was told, I was nothing but trouble – maybe I wasn't a perfectly behaved child, but I *was* just a child. And there are two sides to every story.

At first I would try to explain the reasons for my "bad" behaviour, but my father, who was weighed down with his own troubles, just grew more aggravated. So I learned to accept my punishment in silence. My father wasn't too patient at the best of times and these weren't the best of times. He eventually lost the bakery and was reduced to peddling egg bagels at country markets from a basket around his neck. The new proprietors of the bakery let my father use the still-warm ovens late at night, after they had finished, so he would mix up the dough at home, bake all night, travel all day – sometimes sell his bagels, sometimes not – and come home in a bad mood. All he wanted was a little peace and quiet, so I learned not to waste my energy making explanations that he wasn't interested in hearing. It was easier to just let him add a few whacks to the ones my stepmother had given me, then go and cry in the corner.

As hard as it is to forgive my stepmother for her abuse, I can understand it. She didn't have an easy time of it, living in a rundown flat with a husband who was seldom home, so she took out her frustrations on me. I was another woman's child and had no *chaine*. Besides, she had three children of her own to worry about. The affection she withheld from me, she lavished on my little sisters and brother. Chaitzu was the oldest, and Bella was next, followed by the baby, Simon. My stepmother really loved those kids. She was always hugging and kissing them.

I wasn't jealous – I loved them myself. My greatest pleasure was looking after them when I got home from school. That was one of my jobs. As soon as I walked in the door, my stepmother would say, "Take them outside." She didn't care what we did or where we went as long as I took the children off her hands for a few hours. To me, it wasn't a job; it was a holiday. Being out of the house and away from my stepmother was like being released from prison.

We kept a large open carriage under the front steps, and I would pile the kids inside and push them all over town. That carriage was my bicycle. I'd grease the wheels so it would roll fast, then jump on the back and go for a ride myself. The younger kids would scream and laugh, but Chaitzu was always worried that the carriage would tip over. "Don't go so fast, Erno," she would say. "Mama will get mad." She was always worried about me getting into trouble with my stepmother. When my stepmother beat me, my sisters would cry too.

And that was almost every day.

My stepmother wasn't the only one who picked on me. There was a bully who lived in the same block of flats, a butcher's son who made my life miserable. He was the same age as I was but much bigger and rougher. I was a scrawny, undernourished kid who "played with girls." Whenever the butcher's son encountered me in the courtyard, he would call me a sissy and challenge me to a fight. I wasn't a fighter; I was a runner. But because I had to look after my siblings, I couldn't run. I had to let him push me around until he got tired of the game.

One day, when I was about ten, he really gave me a beating. I ran home crying. When my stepmother saw my battered face, she got very upset. "Don't come home bloody," she said, and gave me a few more shots. By the time my father got home, I had cried myself out and washed myself up. I didn't mention the incident because I knew that I wouldn't get any more sympathy from him than I'd gotten from my stepmother. *Take care of yourself*: that was their attitude. It was hard to accept but understandable. They had enough to worry about without me: Hitler was on the doorstep, my father was working like a horse and barely making a living, and my stepmother was at her wits' end worrying about the "babies." As the older brother, I should be helping them out, not adding to their burden. One of my daily chores was to get water for washing and cooking. We lived in a couple of cramped rooms in a rundown *hoif* (block of flats) in a poor section of town, and there was no running water. Everyone got drinking water from an open well in the middle of the courtyard. The well had a log across the top with a crank and a rope attached to a pail. You cranked the log to lower and raise the pail. It took a lot of cranking. The well was so deep that when you looked down you could barely see the water. As kids we used to each pick a number then drop a stone and count the seconds until we heard a splash.

Once, when I was about seven years old, a cat fell into the well. I remember the health officials coming down to the *hoif* and everyone standing around watching as they brought the drowned cat to the surface. It was a disturbing sight. If a cat can fall into a well, then a seven-year-old boy certainly could.

I didn't mind going for water during the day, but I was scared to death to go at night. Especially during winter, when there was ice all around the well from spilled water. It was hard to crank up a full pail of water and I could slip and fall into the well. Finally, one winter night, I decided to rebel. I can still see my stepmother holding out the pail.

"Go get water."

"It's too dark. I'll go in the morning."

"You'll go when I tell you to go."

"It's too dark."

She slaps me.

"I said get some water."

"No."

My stepmother went crazy. I can still feel her anger. But I was more afraid of the well than I was of being hit, so I just covered my head and tried to protect myself. It was the worst beating I ever took. "Stop, mommy, stop!" my sisters were all crying. Eventually she got tired of hitting me. I crawled into a corner and cried. My sisters tried to comfort me, but my stepmother sent them away.

I didn't get dinner that night. Dinner was usually just a bowl of soup and maybe a potato, but it was my only real meal of the day. Breakfast was a crust of bread, and I never had lunch. I wasn't a big eater, but I was always hungry. I went to bed every night with a half-empty stomach. That night, when I lay down on my straw mattress, it was completely empty.

In the winter, my stepmother and siblings all slept in one large bed, under a feather quilt. I slept on the kitchen floor by the wood stove. The stove would go out during the night and the flat would be ice-cold, but my stepmother never invited me into the big bed. I didn't blame her – I was a bedwetter.

Every night, before I fell asleep, I'd ask God to please wake me if I had to urinate. He usually didn't answer my prayers. I'd get up at dawn, take my mattress outside and hang it over the stair railing, hoping it would be dry by the time everyone else got up. Years later, I learned that I could avoid wetting the bed by keeping my kidneys warm – which is hard to do under a threadbare blanket on the floor of an unheated hovel. Occasionally, my dad would let me sleep at the bakery, on top of the ovens. It was heaven. And I never wet myself.

One winter night when I was about nine, I must have been really shivering because my stepmother took pity on me. "All right," she said, lifting the quilt, "you can come into the bed." "But don't fall asleep," she whispered, as I crawled in beside her. "And don't wake the kids." So I lay there, afraid to move. I was warm but in agony. The string from my pajama bottoms was cutting into my waist. Finally I asked my stepmother if I could loosen it. "No, no!" she said.

So I lay in the dark for what seemed like hours, torn between pain and pleasure.

I remember this incident as if it were yesterday; it was the first time my stepmother treated me like part of the family. And the last....

SINK OR SWIM

Apart from my miserable home life, I had a more or less normal childhood. Bereghovo, a border city of about thirty thousand people, was a nice place to grow up. It had a mild climate, a view of the mountains, rolling countryside, and winding roads leading to orchards, grain farms, and wineries. There were two rivers, the Tisza, which ran through the centre of town, and the Verke, which branched from it. The Tisza was much bigger than the Verke – almost as big as the Duna (or Danube, as it's known outside Europe) – but both rivers had clear blue water and sandy beaches.

Winters were short in Bereghovo and summers were long and warm. Sometimes my father would take us to the beach on his day off. On one of these outings, when I was seven years old, I had a traumatic experience. As usual, my father and stepmother were looking after the other kids and not paying attention to me. I was playing around in the shallow water, crawling along the bottom, pretending to swim. Then I noticed some older kids, a few metres away, jumping in and coming up. I decided to try it. I can still feel the panic.

The water is deeper than it looks – I can't touch bottom.

I come up, gasping for air.

The water is churning around like a whirlpool.

I'm sucked back down.

I come up a second time, coughing and choking.

I see a woman standing on the shore, screaming.

She reaches out to me.

The next thing I remember is waking up on the beach with someone pumping water out of me. By the time my father arrives, I am sitting up.

"What happened?"

I tell him.

He's very upset.

My father wasn't the only one who was upset by my near-drowning. I didn't go in the water for years. All my friends learned to swim before I did. They coaxed me and teased me while I sat on the shore and watched them, nothing could entice me in. Finally, one day, they ganged up on me and tossed me in at a spot where the water was about two metres deep. I remember hitting bottom and pushing myself back to the surface. The river had steep, stone-built banks, but the current was strong so I figured if I could keep from drowning, it would eventually carry me to a spot where I could get out. I flailed around, hitting bottom and pushing myself back up – swimming and drinking, swimming and drinking – until eventually I managed to grab hold of a branch. My clothes were soaked, my stomach hurt, and I was ready to kill all of my so-called friends. But I had learned to swim.

Sink or swim is the story of my life. I was born a runner, not a fighter. What I lacked in size I made up for in speed. But sometimes there's no place to run. I couldn't run from the butcher boy because we lived in the same *hoif.* I had to face him every day when I took my sisters and baby brother outside to play. Every day he teased and taunted me. I couldn't figure him out. What did he want from me? What had I ever done to him? I tried to ignore him, but that just made him more aggressive. This kid made my life hell. He teased me mercilessly and beat me up whenever he felt like it. I was afraid to fight back because he was twice my size. But even a mouse will fight if it has no alternative. One day the butcher boy tied me up in the courtyard and left me there. By the time I managed to untie myself and go home, it was dark, so I got another beating from my stepmother. "That's it," I said to myself. "I'm going to stand up to him even if he kills me."

The next day I'm playing with my sisters in the courtyard when my tormentor walks up, on his way to school. "Oh, you're here," he says, gives me a shove and keeps walking.

"Hey, don't push me," I call after him.

He stops and comes back.

"You want to do something about it?"

All the anger that has been building up in me for years comes out.

I plow into him.

He falls down.

I jump on top of him and kept punching. He is bleeding from the nose and mouth but I'm still hitting him. "Stop it, stop it!" my sisters scream, and they try to pull me off.

Suddenly the storm passes.

I stand up and wait, wondering what he's going to do.

He climbs to his feet, takes one look at me, and runs like hell.

The butcher boy – I've forgotten his name – never tried to bully me again. In fact, I started pushing him around a little. Let's face it, I was no angel either. Eventually we became good friends.

School Daze

I have never made friends easily. Even at school, I felt like an outsider. It had nothing to do with my being Jewish – there were plenty of Jewish kids in my class – it was just my nature. I was shy, introverted, and mistrustful. I felt uncomfortable around people. Things were tough for all the Jewish kids, but most of them had mothers and fathers who loved them. My stepmother considered me a nuisance and my father had no patience for me.

I still remember getting my first report card at the end of Grade one. It's the last day of school and all the kids are jumping around, laughing – they can't wait to run home and show their parents their report cards. So I run home, all excited, and give mine to my father, who has just woken up from his afternoon nap. He takes one look and hands it back.

"What are you showing me – a bunch of C's? And you're happy with this?"

I don't remember showing him another report card.

I wasn't a very attentive student. It's hard to concentrate on an empty stomach. There was a short period of time – in Grade one, I believe – when the school board provided us with milk and buns, but that lasted only a few weeks. When it stopped, I cried. After that, my stepmother would give me a slice of bread – maybe with something on it – before I left for school, and I wouldn't eat again until I came home for dinner. Going without lunch became routine for me. Some kids brought sandwiches in brown paper bags; I would go outside and play soccer, using a rolled-up sock as a ball.

I played soccer at lot, always in bare feet. I never played with shoes on. God forbid, I should scuff them up. My stepmother would kill me. I had only one pair of shoes and they were for special occasions. It wasn't a hardship. None of my friends wore shoes to school. Playing soccer in bare feet was good training. If not for my short temper I could have played for a top team in Canada. But I couldn't get through a practice without getting into a fight. I should have taken up hockey.

Our teachers taught in Hungarian, not Czech because, as I have said, Bereghovo was Czechoslovakian in name only. Every morning schoolchildren sang a patriotic Hungarian song, and in every public building, rather than a picture of the President of Czechoslovakia – Maszarik, a very beloved man with a long handlebar moustache in a business suit – there hung a picture of a distinguished-looking man wearing a fancy Hungarian army uniform and sitting on a horse. I knew nothing about Adolph Hitler at this young age, but Admiral Miklos Horthy, the hero of the Great War, was a familiar figure. In Grade three, several years before I left school, Horthy did come riding into town on his white horse, like the Lone Ranger, and the song we sang every morning came true.

—

In addition to regular school, most of the Jewish kids went to *cheder* (Hebrew school). On Sunday morning and a couple of days a week, after school, I went to a *Talmud Torah* across the street from my uncle's house. Ignac Weissberger, my father's half-brother, was a wood-turner, and his shop was attached to his house. He was the only relative we had in town. I seldom saw him or his married sons, who worked in the business, but my father and I occasionally paid them an unexpected visit.

The atmosphere in *cheder* was more casual than in Hungarian school. In fact, it was a joke. The "teaching" method was a crack on the knuckles with a ruler, a slap on the back of the head, or a well-aimed piece of chalk. Most of our teachers were impatient and bad-tempered. Some were just incompetent. We gave them all nicknames. We called one with a short beard *Kecske* (Goat); another, with a long pipe, was *Bagoshe* (Smoker); another was *Potzok* (Mouse) – I can't remember why.

For generations Jewish children were taught the customs and laws by learned rabbis. In my *cheder* we were taught by a guy who couldn't get a better job. To be a Hebrew teacher in Bereghovo you didn't need a diploma, a love of learning, or a fondness for children. All you needed was a prayer book and a stick.

It's not easy for a kid who has been sitting behind a desk all day to sit still for another few hours, let alone pay attention. In *cheder* we would do anything for a diversion. Between classes one of the older kids, a hustler named Irving Iscovitch, used to walk through the hall selling little packages of chocolate powder. I never had the money to buy, but a few years later, on the "death march," *Itzik* was to sell me something that cost me dearly – an escape plan.

The only kid who paid attention in *cheder* was my best friend, David Jacabovitch. Duni, who sat next to me, was the kind of kid my father would have liked me to be. He had enough *chaine* for both of us. He was not only a top student but outgoing, good-looking, and popular. It was impossible not to like him. He was the kind of son parents dream about.

He had the kind of parents *I* dreamt about. He was the youngest of four brothers in a very close family. His mother sold chickens in the market, and the boys helped her out on weekends. Duni couldn't have wrung a chicken's neck if his life depended on it. In fact, he was so sensitive, he fainted at the sight of blood. His older brothers, Maki and Talian, were a different story. They were nice guys but, if you looked at their little brother the wrong way, you were in trouble – as I found out.

One day in *cheder* I started to push Duni around, and Talian, who was three years older, hit me so hard that my nose started to bleed and wouldn't stop. The blood poured out and the teachers didn't know what to do.

"Let me go to my uncle. He lives across the street."

The teachers are glad to get rid of the problem.

I walk across the street and my uncle comes to the door. When he sees my condition, he calls his sons in from the shop. They apply cold compresses to my neck and call my father. By the time he arrives, the bleeding has stopped.

"What happened?"

I tell him.

He turns and leaves the house.

When I come back to cheder, a few days later, Talian Jacobovitch has a black eye.

Nobody at *cheder* would tell me what happened so I had to put two and two together. I was afraid to ask my father, and he never mentioned the incident again. He didn't have to – his actions spoke for him. Solomon Weisz wasn't going to stand by while his son got picked on. A few years later, in Auschwitz, the shoe would be on the other foot.

—

My father wasn't the only adult who stuck up for me. In my last year at school I had a very nice teacher, a Jewish woman with no family of her own. She knew about my home situation and couldn't help noticing that I never brought lunch to school. One day she invited me to her place for dinner. I was shy about going, but not shy enough to turn down food.

She lived by herself in a small room. After feeding me, she talked to me about my stepmother.

"What you are going through is part of life, Erno. And life is tough. I'd like to help you, but I don't have much myself."

I was touched by her kindness but unable to respond. I didn't know how to behave with adults, so I just listened, politely, thanked her for dinner, and left. She invited me back a few more times but I remained tongue-tied. To this day I feel bad about not being able to express my gratitude to this good-hearted woman who tried to make my life a little easier. I don't even remember her name. And there's probably nobody left to light a memorial candle in her memory. My Grade five teacher is just one of the six million *parasites* the saviour of Germany exterminated to keep the blood of his people "pure."

BLOODLESS INVASION

In the spring of 1939, the song we sang in school every morning came true. Miklos Horthy, having made a deal with the devil, came riding into town on his white horse. In a futile attempt to avoid war, the Allied Nations had let Hitler take back the *Sudetenland* (the "German" part of Czechoslovakia) and, in a futile attempt to keep Stalin in check, Hitler had given Horthy the green light to take back the "Hungarian" part. Without firing a shot, Hungary took back most of the territory she had lost in the First World War: an area at the foot of the Carpathian Mountains known as the *Carpaski Ruse*.

The city fathers welcomed the "liberators" with open arms. I remember standing in the middle of a cheering crowd as the Hungarian cavalry, in fancy green uniforms and feathered hats, paraded down the street with banners flying and sabres clanking. A short time later, the name of the city was changed from Bereghovo to Beregszasz.

Otherwise, it was business as usual.

Even before he marched into Poland, Hitler was implementing his plan to make Europe *Judenrein* (clean of Jews), but his poison was slow in spreading to Hungary. The start of the war barely affected my daily life. It was miserable before, and it remained miserable. I occasionally heard my father talking politics with his left-wing cronies, and saw him secretly listening to forbidden newscasts from the West, but that was his business.

Prior to the takeover, my father didn't concern himself much with the antics of the barbarians who had risen to power in Germany. After all, he was a citizen of a modern democratic nation with no history of religious persecution. He had spent the happiest years of his life in the service of his country. Then suddenly his country was pulled out from under his feet and he found himself standing on alien soil.

Shortly after the Hungarians took over, I remember my father driving the family by horse and wagon to a little town called Mihalovce, which was still in Czechoslovakia. I don't know how long we stayed there. The next thing I remember is being back in Beregszasz with just my stepmother and siblings, my father having been drafted into the Hungarian army. From the ages of nine to eleven, everything happened so fast – bang, bang, bang – that the picture I have of those years is not clear.

Apparently, during the first years of the war, Hungary had maintained a "neutral" position. Horthy sat on the fence, waiting to see which side would come out on top. Every time the balance shifted, Hungary leaned in that direction. When Hitler started throwing his weight around, the Hungarian Regent would replace a West-leaning prime minister with a more zealous advocate of "racial purity" – only to reinstall a moderate as soon as the pressure relaxed. Horthy was allowed to drag his feet on "the Jewish Question" because Hitler needed Hungary as a buffer between Germany and the Soviet Union. In exchange for the Carpaski Ruse, Hungary had agreed to send thousands of well-trained troops into the Ukraine to defend the Eastern front.

Hitler expected Horthy's crack army to defeat Stalin's ragtag troops in a matter of weeks, if not days. But the weeks dragged into months, the losses mounted, and finally, in one decisive battle, Hungary's army was wiped out and the German Fuehrer no longer had any reason to treat his "friend" with kid gloves. He gave Horthy an ultimatum: implement the "Final Solution" under Nazi supervision or implement it under German *occupation*. Horthy quickly jumped off the fence, dissolved Hungary's moderate government, and installed the "Crossed-Arrow" party, an ultra-nationalist regime that modelled itself on the Third Reich.

I, of course, learned these things years later. As a boy, politics was not my big concern. I knew there was a war going on, but it had yet to affect me personally. There were no bombs falling on Beregszasz. The only fighting I saw was between cowboys and Indians.

One of the positive things I remember about the Hungarian takeover is that they were big in the movie industry. I remember a very funny actor, Lotabar Kalman, who was like a Hungarian Bob Hope. Sometimes my friends would sneak me into the theatre to see him. We had a nice theatre in town and every seat was numbered. A policeman would walk around, checking tickets, so I'd hide in the bathroom until the movie started, then try to find an empty seat.

Most of the movies were Hungarian, but some-times they showed an American movie. I remember seeing Gary Cooper in one of his first films. He ran around the jungle, catching people with his lasso. Another big movie was *Gulliver's Travels*. I really wanted to see those Lilliputians, but the theatre was always sold out.

Even when I had to start wearing a yellow arm-band, I wasn't concerned. All my friends were wearing them. One day we were told to go to a certain place

– a police station or government building – and pick up the armbands. Or maybe the teacher handed them out; I don't remember. You wore it on your left arm. It was just something I slipped on every morning and forgot about. But there's a saying: *If you forget you're a Jew, a Gentile will remind you.*

Once a week, after school, we had "scouts." The scout leaders marched us up and down the schoolyard like young soldiers. I didn't mind – I liked drilling. But one day, after we had lined up, the leader said that everyone whose name he called should step out of line and move to the left.

He calls out the names of all the Jewish kids.

There are about forty of us, all wearing yellow armbands.

We are split into smaller groups and marched away. My group is marched to the city hall, which has a large courtyard paved with cobblestones. Weeds and grass are growing between the stones. Our new drill leader gives us an order.

"Clean it up."

"With what?"

"Your hands."

We all spend the next few hours on our knees, pulling out grass and weeds.

That became my weekly routine. If there were no grounds to clean up, they would march us into a field, hand us shovels, and make us dig ditches. Some of the leaders didn't push us too hard; others enjoyed being cruel. Instead of marching after school, the Jewish "scouts" would be forced to perform menial labour, but to maintain the illusion we were allowed to wear our scout caps.

I wore mine every day. It was the only new article of clothing I had to wear and I can still picture it: olive green like my father's uniform, with a metal badge in the red, white, and green colours of the Hungarian flag. My Hungarian scout cap was the first thing I put on in the morning and the last thing I took off at night. It saved me from combing my hair.

And it saved my life.…

Exile

One day in the summer of 1941, a policeman showed up at our door. We had been expecting him. The news was all over town that Jewish non-citizens were being deported. My stepmother fell into this category. Marrying my father hadn't changed her status; she was still considered a resident alien. She had been contacted by the authorities and told to pack her belongings.

Something you can carry.

My stepmother had run around like a chicken without a head making bundles from sheets, pillow-cases – anything she could find – and they were sitting on the floor when the city policeman arrived. He was young and very polite. He had nothing against Jews; he was just doing his job.

"These people are to come with me."

He reads out the names of my stepmother and her children, who are all listed under her maiden name, Simkovitch.

"What about him?" my stepmother asks, tossing her head in my direction.

The policeman looks at me.

"Who is he?"

"Weisz, Erno."

The policeman looks at the sheet of paper.

"He's not on the list."

"Maybe it's on another page."

The policeman looks and looks but can't find my name.

My stepmother becomes hysterical.

"What am I supposed to do? He's my stepson."

The policeman doesn't know what to say to this pretty young woman who doesn't look any more Jewish than he does.

"Where is the boy's father?"

"He's in the army."

The policeman looks surprised.

"He's Hungarian?"

My stepmother shakes her head.

"Czechoslovakian. He's a citizen."

"Well, that's why his son isn't on the list. He can stay."

"Stay? How can he stay here all by himself? He's eleven years old!"

"Doesn't he have any relatives he can live with?"

My stepmother makes a face.

"My worst enemies should have such relatives. Besides, what about my children; you think I can carry them on my back, together with those bundles?"

The policeman leaves it up to me.

"Do you want to go with your stepmother?"

I don't know what to say, so I say nothing.

The policeman, noticing my cap, tries to make friends.

"I see you're in the scouts."

My stepmother answers for me.

"He used to be in the scouts. Now he's a weed-puller with a fancy cap that he never takes off his head!"

The policeman looks at her with new eyes. Maybe this tiny woman isn't as sweet and helpless as she looks. He shrugs his shoulders.

"Okay, if you want him to come, take him along."

―

He gave my stepmother half an hour to pack some last-minute things – food, pots, pans – so she untied all the bundles, took some things out, put other things in, and made new bundles. Some she made small enough for my little sisters to carry. Shimon was too young to carry anything – he had just started walking.

After she had retied the bundles, my stepmother took her children into the bedroom and closed the door behind her. I could hear her talking, but I couldn't make out what she said.

The door opens and she comes out, with tears in her eyes. She kneels down and starts hugging and kissing my baby brother and sisters. Tears are rolling down her cheeks. I can hardly hold back my own tears. I love these kids. They're closer to me than my "real" sister. I can't even remember what Szidi looks like. The last time I saw her, she was a baby.

The policeman is getting uncomfortable.

"If you're packed, we'd better get going."

At the police station we were put in a large room filled with other people and their bundles of belongings. The door was left unlocked. The adults sat there with worried looks while the kids ran around, playing. After a few hours, we were loaded onto buses and driven to the railways station, where a passenger train was waiting.

We board the train and everyone puts their bundles on the racks, or on the seat beside them, or on the floor – wherever there's an empty space. The whistle blows, the train gives a lurch, and we are on our way to the Ukraine.

It was a short distance but a long trip. Beregszasz was just a few hundred kilometres from the eastern border, but it took all day to get there. We kept stopping and picking up more passengers. At every station Jewish people stood on the platform, handing up food and drink, wishing us good luck, crying.

I remember getting a sandwich – a rye bread sandwich. I can still taste it. I couldn't understand why these people were being so generous. I didn't appreciate what was happening to us. To me, eating was a celebration. The memory of strangers handing up food remains a pleasant one.

Other memories are not so pleasant.

After travelling all day in relative comfort on the train, we come to a stop in the middle of nowhere. A Hungarian soldier tells us to pick up our bundles – the rest of the journey will be on foot.

I pick up my bundle and get out with everyone else.

There are about four hundred of us and it's pitch black outside.

We walk for hours in the dark, but we are allowed to go at our own pace and my bundle isn't too heavy.

Finally it begins to get light and I see a river in the distance.

As we come closer, someone identifies the river as the Dnieper, the border with the Ukraine. It's a wide river and I see a high bridge across it up ahead. But the soldiers are marching us away from the bridge rather than toward it. I wonder why. As we come closer, I see that the bridge has been bombed out. We are being marched to a floating bridge, farther down the bank. Motorboats were moving slowly up and down the river between the floating bridge and the bombed-out bridge. Every once in a while the boats, piloted by Hungarian soldiers, would stop so that the soldiers could pull something out of the water into the boat. These were not small objects but heavy things that took two of them to lift.

The march has slowed to a crawl. No one seems to want to keep walking. People are just standing there, staring at the water. I look around and see my step-mother talking to another woman. The woman grabs her head and starts moaning.

"Oy vay's mir (oh, my God)! Oy vays's mir!"

Suddenly people are crying and screaming.

What's going on?

I look at the river and am now close enough to see what the men in the boats are fishing for – the bloated bodies of men, women, and children, floating on their backs.

—

Our predecessors had been turned over to the Ukrainian militia (local peasants who had been given an armband and a rifle) to continue the march to the next town or village, but the crafty Ukrainians had found an easier way to carry out their task. They would simply line up "the Jews" along the riverbank and shoot them. The bodies wouldn't even have to be buried on Ukrainian soil – they would fall into the river and be carried downstream into Hungary. But the bombed-out bridge spoiled their plan. When the Hungarian soldiers arrived with a new batch of deportees, dozens of bodies were tangled up behind the pylons. The soldiers were horrified. If these bodies floated back into Hungary, everyone would think *they* had committed this atrocity. So they got motorboats and started fishing the bodies out of the water.

When they turned the new deportees over to the Ukrainian militia, it was at the point of a rifle, with an ultimatum:

"You shoot them, we shoot you!"

Of course none of us knew about the ultimatum when we arrived at the border. Most people around me fully expected to end up floating in the river with their fellow ex-patriot Ukrainian Jews. And no amount of reassurance from our Hungarian escorts could change that belief. The adult deportees had to be coaxed, cajoled, and almost dragged across the floating bridge.

But I was just a backward eleven-year-old who had no idea what was going on. And my stepmother didn't take time to discuss the situation with me. Unlike her, I didn't know that to some Ukrainian peasants, "Jews" were on the same level as farm animals. So when the Hungarian soldiers said, "Go ahead, you'll be all right," I believed them.

⸺

Our Ukrainian escorts were much rougher than the Hungarians. And they spoke a "foreign" language. As soon as we crossed the river, the leader of the militia made us sit down and listen to a long speech. I only caught bits and pieces, but I'm sure my stepmother understood every word. I didn't ask her what he said and she didn't tell me. When the speech finally ended, they got us to our feet and started marching us down a dusty country road.

—

We are no longer walking at our own pace – this is a forced march. They keep pushing and pushing, marching us faster. Every time we come to a village, our guards are replaced, and the new guys, in a hurry to get to their own village, pick up the pace. My "light" bundle feels like it's full of stones. I kept changing it from one side to the other. My back is beginning to ache like a sore tooth.

We passed a few wagons along the way, but the drivers didn't pay any more attention to us than to cattle being driven down a country road to the slaughterhouse. I overheard people talking about what had happened to the previous deportees, and this revelation weighed more heavily on me than my bundle. The Ukrainians were taking us away from the river because they were afraid to shoot us in front of the Hungarian soldiers. As soon as they found a suitable spot – like a forest – we would all be killed.

—

We march until it starts to get dark, then stop at a stone enclosure that stands in a field like a castle with no roof.

"This is where you're going to stay the night," the guard says and walks away.

We all put down our bundles and make a place on the ground.

After we are settled, my stepmother runs around asking questions.

The Ukrainian guards reassure her.

"Don't worry. You'll get up in the morning, have something to eat, and march further."

She comes back, takes some food from one of the bundles, feeds my siblings, and gives me a piece of bread or something.

But I have no appetite. I'm too upset and depressed to eat.

The kids fell asleep as soon as their heads hit the ground. They were exhausted. I was also exhausted, but I couldn't fall asleep. Every time I closed my eyes, I saw those bodies floating in the river. So I just lay there looking up at the stars, which I thought I might be seeing for the last time.

—

I hear noises. Voices. Laughter. I sit up. In the darkness I see militiamen. They are going around with rifles, making people open their bags. "You won't need this," they say and help themselves to some article of clothing. Or jewellery. Or whatever else appeals to them. I lie back down and close my eyes, but I can't close my ears. I hear them say it, over and over — "you won't need this, you won't need this" — like it's a big joke.

—

I awoke at sunrise, soaking wet — and not just from the dew. I didn't care. Bedwetting was the least of my worries. The laughing thieves had dispelled any doubts that we were marching to our deaths. I was sorry they hadn't taken any of my stepmother's junk. My bundle felt twice as heavy as it had the day before. And the longer we walked, the heavier it became. Why lug these pots and pans we were never going to use?

I started complaining to my stepmother, but she ignored me. I was walking slower and slower. "Come on, come on!" she would scream whenever I fell behind. At every new town, there were different guys with rifles who always picked up the pace. I don't know how many towns we passed through. I just remember walking, carrying the parcel, crying, and watching my stepmother, who was hysterical most of the time. We'd walk all day then stop for night in a farmer's field or barn. Within a few days, we ran out of food, as did everyone else.

As soon as we were settled, my stepmother would disappear for an hour and come back with something for her children to eat. She'd also give me a morsel.

People started whispering. One day, during the march, a woman came up to me and told me what everyone was whispering about.

"Your mother is sleeping with the farmers in exchange for food."

It hit me like a fist in the stomach. What kind of person would say such a thing to a child? I didn't believe this malicious gossip. She was just envious, I thought. Years later, I realized the woman was probably telling the truth. My stepmother would have done anything for her children.

Sometimes, when we stopped for the night, a farmer would show up and hand around slices of bread. "Give to *malinka* (little ones)," he would say. In Auschwitz, I would discover that even a Nazi SS officer could have a soft spot for children.

My stepmother was so worried about her own children that she didn't have any patience for my suffering. All I wanted was a little attention or reassurance, but when I complained about the weight of my bundle, she just became angry. Not knowing how much longer I had to carry the bundle, my ordeal seemed endless. Finally, on the third or fourth day, when we stopped for a rest, I came to a decision.

"I'm not going to carry it any more."

My stepmother doesn't look at me.

"You'll carry it."

"No, I won't. It's too heavy."

She turns and glares at me.

"You'll carry it."

"No, I won't."

She tried to bully me, but I wouldn't budge.

She went crazy.

"Go to hell! Get away from me! I don't want to look at you."

I moved away a few feet.

She untied my bundle and started sorting through the stuff to see what she had to get rid of.

She looks up and sees me watching her.

She starts to scream again.

"Get out of my sight! Go away so I can't see you!"

I disappear into the crowd.

—

It was such a relief to have the burden removed that I felt like a newborn. But I wanted to be with my siblings so I kept sneaking up behind them. As soon as my stepmother caught sight of me, she'd start screaming, so I finally gave up. From time to time, some of the older marchers would fall down and the guards would prod them back to their feet. No one had to prod me. Without that bundle I could have walked forever. The longer we walked, the better I felt. Maybe we weren't going to be shot after all.

We marched another few days – I don't remember how long – then one afternoon I saw buildings in the distance. "That's Kholomaya," someone said, and people around me started cheering.

—

The streets of Kholomaya are crowded with pedestrians and military vehicles carrying soldiers to and from the Eastern front. The Hungarians have sustained heavy losses. Some of the soldiers are on crutches or wearing bandages. I am walking down the road and no guard is pushing me. I look around. They have all disappeared. People are slowing down and stopping to rest. I keep walking. I'm not tired; I'm hungry. Eventually, I'm walking by myself.

—

I passed a few houses with vegetable gardens and my mouth started to water. But it was broad daylight and the street was full of people. I would have to come back at night if I wanted to raid these gardens. While I was walking down the sidewalk, wondering which way to go, I saw a young couple watching me. Their clothes were nice but shabby and they were wearing yellow stars. They approached me and the man addressed me in Yiddish.

"Where are you from, young man?"

"Beregszasz."

"Oh, Hungary."

"Yes."

"Where are you going?"

"I don't know. I just got here."

"Where are your parents?"

"My father is in the army and my mother is dead. I have a stepmother."

I tell them the story.

The woman can't believe it.

"Where are you going to sleep?"

"I don't know."

She looks at her husband. He nods. She turns back to me.

"Come with us."

—

The couple took me to their small apartment and fed me. They didn't have much to eat, but they shared what they had. That night I slept in a real bed. I asked God to please wake me in case of an emergency and, for once, my prayers were answered. I went to the washroom twice during the night and woke up in a dry bed.

The next morning at breakfast the couple told me about their situation. The husband had lost his job – no Jewish people were working – and they were living from hand to mouth.

"We don't know what's going to happen to us, but you can stay here if you like."

"Thank you."

"Would you like to go outside now?"

"Sure."

—

I walked around all day looking for gardens that I could come back to at night. Then suddenly I saw my stepmother about a block away, standing on a corner waiting to cross the street.

—

She turns and looks at me but gives no sign of recognition.

Did she see me?

Should I wave to her? Call out?

As I stand there, debating with myself, the light changes.

My stepmother walks across the street.

And out of my life.

—

I would never find out whether my stepmother had recognized me that day. But as I continued to walk around, I noticed that several Hungarian soldiers were looking at me as if my face were familiar. Finally one of them approached me, and I discovered that it wasn't my face he recognized.

"Where did you get that cap?"

"In Beregszasz."

"Is that where you live?"

"Yes."

"So what are you doing in Kholomaya?"

"They marched a whole bunch of us in yesterday."

"Who marched you?"

I told him about the deportation. He couldn't believe his ears. The soldiers on the Eastern front had been away from Hungary for months and had no idea what was going on back home. I explained that I was deported because my stepmother was not a Hungarian citizen.

"So why are you on your own?"

"My stepmother doesn't like me. She chased me away."

I explain about the bundle.

"What about your father, where is he?"

"In the army."

"The Hungarian army?"

"Yes."

"Where is he stationed?"

"Buchahesa."

"Sixty-six?"

The 66th regiment was a non-combat unit to which the few Jewish soldiers who had yet to be discharged from the army were assigned. My father, who had been stripped of his rank, was doing some kind of menial work in a medical clinic. The soldier I spoke to was familiar with the regiment, but everything else I told him was a revelation. He kept shaking his head in disbelief. Finally he told me to wait on the sidewalk. He returned to the bar, which he'd just left, and came back with another soldier who had three pips on his collar. The first soldier brought his sergeant over to me.

"Tell him what you told me."

I repeat the story.

The sergeant is astounded. He can't believe Hungary is deporting the Jews.

"What's going on back home? Have they all gone crazy?"

He looks at me for a long time. Then he turns to his friend.

"How can we help him?"

They walked away and had a short conference. When they came back, my friend the soldier did the talking.

"Can you be here tomorrow afternoon?"

"I guess so."

"Don't guess, you be here. Tomorrow at two o'clock. Right on this spot."

"Okay. Why?"

"See that hospital across the street? At two o'clock tomorrow they're evacuating a bunch of wounded men back to Hungary. We'll try and get you into one of the ambulances."

—

The Jewish couple was very happy for me. And I was glad I didn't have to "take the bread out of their mouths." They offered me dinner, but I said the soldiers had fed me – which wasn't true. After the couple went to bed, I snuck out and raided a garden.

I can still taste those fresh vegetables. To this day, I love cucumbers.

After I had stuffed myself with cucumbers and tomatoes, I went back to the couple's house, but I didn't go inside. I didn't want to disturb them. Instead I decided to spend the night in the shed they had out back. I fell asleep immediately on the dirt floor. I was so tired I could have slept on a stone.

The next morning I got up at sunrise, but I didn't go in the house. I didn't want the couple to have to share their food with me. The previous night I had thanked them and said goodbye, telling them that the soldiers were going to give me breakfast. I started walking around the town, trying to kill time. My stomach was churning, not only from cucumbers but from excitement. I was torn between happiness and fear. The soldiers hadn't sugar-coated the pill they'd fed me. If you were caught trying to cross the border without papers, you were as good as dead. The border guards between the Ukraine and Hungary were an elite unit of the Nylas, Hungary's version of the Gestapo. They were completely ruthless. If they found me in the ambulance, they wouldn't ask about my Hungarian scout cap, they would just put me up against a tree and shoot me.

I walked the streets for what seemed like a year, waiting for two o'clock to arrive. Finally it did.

The soldiers met me at the appointed spot. About a dozen ambulances were lined up along the curb. I waited with one soldier while the other went to talk to the ambulance drivers. He approached one who shook his head. He approached a few other drivers with the same result. Finally one of the drivers looked in my direction and nodded. The soldier waved me over. I walked to the ambulance on shaking legs. The driver spoke to me without looking at me.

"I can't guarantee you'll survive this trip. My life might be in danger, too. But if you're willing to risk your life, I'll take a chance. I'll tell the guys who are riding with you to put a blanket over you before we get to the border."

"Can I get in now?"

"No, I'll tell you when."

I walk away and wait. My heart is pounding.

Finally he waves me over.

"Okay, get in."

He is standing at the back, holding the door open. Inside there are two benches, one on either side of the vehicle. I climb between the benches and sit down on the floor.

Almost immediately two wounded soldiers follow me into the ambulance – one on crutches, with a bandage on his head, the other on a stretcher. Neither seems surprised to see me. The mobile soldier sits down on one side and the stretcher is laid down on the other side. The stretcher-bearers must be aware of the plan because they too ignore me.

The door is slammed shut.

We pull away.

The soldier on the stretcher looks to me for the first time.

"If you get tired, lie down. We'll cover you with a blanket."

There wasn't much conversation as we drove west, toward the border. The soldier who was sitting up was even less talkative than the one on the stretcher. As we bumped down one country road after another, I began to feel drowsy. I fought to stay awake. I was afraid to fall asleep. But I could hardly keep my eyes open ...

I woke up with the blanket over my face. We weren't moving. The driver was talking to someone outside the vehicle.

It must be the border guard.

Please, let him wave us through.

I hear the sound of heavy boots walking around the ambulance.

The back door opens with a bang, and a shaft of sunlight shines through the blanket.

I shut my eyes and hold my breath.

The border guard shouts something to the driver.

The driver shouts back.

The back door slams shut.

The motor roars and we start to move.

I count the seconds – one, two, three....

After one minute, I let out my breath and take a gasp of air.

By two minutes I'm breathing normally.

I count off another minute then pull the blanket away from my face.

I'm soaked with sweat.

The two soldiers are smiling.

REPATRIATION

"**O**kay, we're in Hungary. You get out here."

As I climbed out of the back of the ambulance, I saw that it had stopped at the intersection of two country roads. The driver called me over and pointed to the branch I was to take.

"That's the road into Okormezo. Just keep walking and you'll come to a railway station. Tell them you want to go to your dad. Tell the conductor 'Buchahesa.'"

I thanked him and said goodbye to the two soldiers.

They wished me luck, and the ambulance drove away.

I started walking. The day was dull and cloudy and looked like rain. On both sides of the road were deep ditches that forced me to walk on the travelled portion of the road. I worried that a policeman would stop me, but there was no traffic in sight.

After I'd walked for a while I thought I heard someone call my name.

Weisz!

I stopped and looked around. Who could be calling me out here? There were a few houses beside the road, but they were a long way off. It must be my imagination. I started walking again. Again I heard my name, louder this time.

"Weisz Erno!"

It was a man's voice, coming from behind me.

I turn around and see a wagon.

The driver is my cousin Abrish, who has a dairy farm in the area.

He can't believe his eyes.

"So it is you," he says, stopping the wagon. "How on Earth did you get here?"

"An ambulance brought me."

"An ambulance?"

I explain about the soldiers sneaking me out of Kholomaya.

He can't understand it.

"Why were you deported? Your father is a citizen."

"It's a long story."

"Climb up. You'll tell me on the way home."

I told him the whole story as we drove to his farm and then repeated it at the dinner table. The family gave me an unexpectedly warm welcome, feeding me and fussing over me. I wasn't used to such treatment. After dinner, they started whispering among themselves.

I began to feel even more self-conscious. Why were they whispering? Finally Abrish came up to me.

"We're going to buy you a ticket to Buchahesa."
I didn't know what to say. I was flabbergasted by this generosity from people who didn't have a good word to say about my father. While one of my cousins went to buy the ticket, they coached me on what to do and say.

"This is a border town and it's swarming with gendarmes. If they see an eleven-year -old wandering around, they'll ask for your identity card. So watch out for them."

One of my cousins got me a jacket.
"Here, put this on."

It fits quite well – and it doesn't have a yellow arm-band.

Abrish arrives with my ticket.
"We'll delay our departure as long as possible."

He hands me the ticket.

I put it in the pocket of my new jacket and sit on pins and needles until it's time to go.

Abrish accompanies me.

—

The train is already standing in the station.

There are no police in sight.

Abrish turns to me.

"Okay, it's time to go."

I thank him, say goodbye, walk across the platform, and board the train.

A man is sitting in the compartment.

I sit down across from him.

He smiles.

I decide to take a chance.

"Will you let me know when we get to Buchahesa? My father is there."

He nods.

"Oh yeah, sixty-six."

The train trip was short, just a few hours. The conductor stuck his head into the compartment a couple of times but didn't ask to see my ticket. He saw a young kid travelling alone and put two and two together. The man told me where to get off, but I didn't know where to go after that, so I approached a man on the street for directions.

It isn't far, he tells me.

He was right. I had no trouble finding the army base. I'd heard my father was working in a clinic – as a janitor or something – and when I saw the word *Medical* on one of the buildings I started to cry.

I walked up to the door with tears running down my face. A man in uniform stopped me just inside the door.

"What do you want?"

"I'm looking for my father."

I can tell he doesn't believe me. Later, this officer told my father that he thought I was one of the street urchins who were always coming into the building to beg, borrow, or steal something. He is a Jewish doctor. I can tell from the three dark spots on his collar where his captain's stars have been removed.

"What's your father's name?"

"Weisz Solomon."

The officer grabs his head like he's just been hit. He looks at me excitedly.

"Wait here."

He runs down the hall and comes back a few seconds later, grinning.

"Walk behind me so he can't see you."

I follow the man down the hall like a shadow. He stops at a flight of stairs and sings out:

"Weisz Bacsi, I've got a present for you."

My father, who is halfway up the stairs, turns around. When he sees me, he runs down the stairs so fast he almost falls on his face. He grabs me and starts hugging and kissing me. He is so overcome with emotion that he can't speak. When he finally finds his voice, he starts firing questions like a machine gun.

"What happened? Why are you here? Where is your stepmother? How are the kids? Are they still all alive?"

I told my father all about the deportation. I didn't hold anything back. Satisfied that the rest of his family was still alive, he took me into the doctor's office and fed me.

Then he starts asking questions again.

I tell him the whole story.

By this time, word of my arrival has spread through the hospital, and everyone in the building is standing at the door, listening.

I feel like a movie star.

I'm not used to being the centre of attention.

—

I got used to it. Over the next few weeks, my father, who was sick with worry, kept asking me questions. He was very patient and understanding. He didn't blame me for refusing to carry the bundle – even though, looking back, it seems like a very selfish thing to do. But I was just a kid. To me, my stepmother wasn't a young woman with small children to look after but a resourceful adult who went out of her way to make my life miserable. It was a question of self-preservation. I knew my stepmother would do anything to protect her own kids, and since she didn't seem to care whether I lived or died, I had to look after myself.

But now my father was watching me like a mother hen. He wouldn't let me out of his sight. On the day after my arrival, I was sitting in the outhouse when suddenly I heard a pounding. I opened the door to find my father standing there with a concerned look.

"What are you doing in here? I've been looking for you for two hours."

I smile foolishly.

"I fell asleep."

I expected him to scold me. Instead, he started laughing. It was wonderful to have my father laugh at my shenanigans. The time I spent with him in the clinic was like a holiday. One of the officers had a bicycle, and I taught myself to ride, the biggest thrill of my life. I rode that bicycle up and down the streets all day. I also made friends with some of the local kids who hung around the clinic. One of them sold candies to the soldiers, and I became his best customer. I was given money left and right. Everyone treated me like a son. I was a substitute for their own children, whom they hadn't seen or heard from in months.

My father, meanwhile, was out of his mind with worry. He kept asking me questions about Beregszasz. He'd been away for more than a year and was hungry to hear anything I could tell him. I was very open with him. I even told him about my stepmother's "friend" – a young guy who used to hang around our *hoif* and occasionally sleep over.

That, my father didn't want to hear.

His menial duties didn't take up much of my father's time, so we spent a good deal of time together.. In spite of his constant state of anxiety, he never scolded me. Life was very pleasant. When I wasn't with my father, I was riding the bicycle, hanging around with my new friends, and eating candy. It seemed too good to last. And it was. After a few weeks, my father broke the bad news.

"You can't stay here forever. They might discharge me any day now. When I get back home, I'll send for you – in the meantime I want you to stay with *Zindli Bacsi* (Uncle Zindli)."

My maternal uncle, Zindli Blau, was my mother's big brother. He owned a large grain farm outside a village called Tarpa, about forty-five kilometres from Bereghovo. Uncle Zindli was considerably older than my mother – the baby of the family – and had more or less taken over as head of the family. Several of his married daughters and two grown sons lived at home, and my maternal *zaida* (grandfather) – a devout watchmaker with a long, reddish-grey beard – lived on the third floor. But it was a large house with plenty of room. Zindli's wife even had a little grocery store at the front of it.

Like all my mother's relatives, Uncle Zindli had no use for my freethinking father, and this feeling extended to me. He referred to both of us as *Goyim* (Gentiles). Still, he had agreed to take me in. You can't have too many hands on a farm at harvest time. And maybe he thought his family's influence would help turn his prodigal nephew into a "good Jew."

I arrived in September just before the High Holidays. On the evening of *Rosh Hashanah* (Jewish New Year), my aunt gave me some nice clothes to wear and I went to the synagogue with the family. I liked my nice clothes and didn't feel out of place. The services were just a few hours long and I enjoyed myself.

But the next morning we had to go to the synagogue again, and the services lasted past lunchtime. We went home for a few hours; then returned in the evening. The novelty was beginning to wear off. Seven days later, it was *Yom Kippur* (the Day of Atonement) and we stayed in the synagogue all day. I was bored to tears. While my elders sat in the sanctuary, asking God to forgive their sins, I snuck out.

I wasn't alone. The corridor was filled with kids wandering around, trying to kill time. I noticed a couple of boys about my age, standing in a corner.

I walked over to see what they were doing.

I couldn't believe my eyes.

These nicely dressed kids were urinating against the wall.

"What are you doing?"

"You do it too."

Just then the synagogue shamas (beadle) walked up to us. When he saw what we were doing, he was shocked. "How could you do such a thing?" he asked me. I didn't bother to explain that I was as shocked as he was. It was easier just to accept a patch (slap) in the behind.

I was grateful this story never got back to my uncle Zindli because it would have absolutely destroyed our relationship. I lived in his house and worked in the fields with his children for quite a while, and he treated me like part of the family. I wasn't crazy about farm work, though, and my uncle, who was a bit of a joker, liked to tease me.

"You better get up early. Tomorrow we have to cut down the thistle."

Cutting thistle was the job I hated the most. You harvest grain sitting on a machine, but the weeds have to be cleared by hand. We would walk up and down the rows, carrying a stick with a blade on the end of it, and cut down the thistle. I wasn't very good at it, so my cousins would follow me around. "You missed one," they would say – and I'd go back and cut it down. They had acres of land and it took forever to clear it.

Then the thresher came in – or maybe it's called a combine – a huge machine that cut down the grain, separated it, and put it in sacks. A few stalks always fell on the ground and we had to walk over the harvested field with big rakes and gather them up. One day, when I was busy raking a section they had assigned to me, my cousins were ready to go to lunch.

"C'mon, it's time to eat."

"Go ahead. I'll be there as soon as I finish this section."

They drove off and left me. I could have sat down to rest, but instead I kept going. I wasn't crazy about farm work, but I was a good worker –no one had to push me. If I had a job to do, I did it. When I finally finished my section and went back to the house, I was rewarded for my effort.

"I just heard from your dad," my uncle said. "He's home."

I went straight to the bedroom and packed my few belongings. My uncle had treated me well, but I wasn't sorry to leave. I missed my father. And I wouldn't miss the hard work.

My father and I were strangers in our hometown. For months we walked the streets of Beregszasz looking for work. The longer we looked, the lower my father's spirits sank. As a young man, he had been a bit of a vagabond but he was never a "bum." All his life he had worked hard and taken pride in his work. Even when he was baking egg bagels at home and selling them from a basket around his neck, he knew they were the *best* egg bagels. Now he couldn't get a job in his own bakery.

I couldn't understand it.

"But your name is on the window."

"I guess my name is still worth something," he said. "When I went into the army, I rented my bakery licence to a Gentile for peanuts."

When my father joined the army, a Jew was still allowed to operate a business. But times had changed. As the tide of war turned against him, Hitler had stepped up the pace of the "Final Solution." Hungary was trying to protect itself from invasion by implementing the policies of Nazi Germany, and the Gentile who now operated my father's business was afraid to hire him, even as a worker. The few dollars the man paid in rent was all we had to live on.

My father had rented a room from a poor widow with three daughters. He had to pay extra for my board, which was another burden. The prodigal son was now a millstone around his neck. My father didn't know what to do with me. "You can't send him to school," the widow told him. "He was deported."

"But my name wasn't on the list," I said.

My father didn't say anything – he just listened. All the life had gone out of him. We slept in the same bed, lived in the same room, but seldom said anything to one another. He no longer asked me about my step-mother. There was nothing more I could tell him. We heard that the Jews in Kholomaya had been taken into the forest in Kamenecs Podolsk and killed.

I bummed around all day with other kids who had nothing better to do. There was never any shortage of kids on the street –where there was one, there would soon be five. I'd hang around the ice cream store, sneak into the movies, look for bicycles. I wasn't in-terested in girls; riding a bicycle was my biggest thrill. Occasionally I'd deliver newspapers, earning a few cents, which I saved up and used to buy cigarettes for my father. Having nothing to smoke was as hard on my father as having nothing to eat, and going without food was much harder on him than on me.

I was used to walking around with a half-empty stomach. When I was lucky enough to get a decent meal, I ate just enough to stop the hunger pangs and saved the rest for later. My father was a different story. He wasn't used to going without food, coffee, and cigarettes, not to mention having a twelve-year-old son hanging around his neck like a stone. Not only could he not feed and clothe me properly; he couldn't tolerate my behaviour. I tried to make the best of our situation and go on with my life, but my father had no life to go on with. He'd lost his young wife, his adorable children, and his livelihood. He'd been stripped of everything but his pride, and he ended up swallowing *that*.

—

Citrom Yakov (Jacob Citrom) was the head of the local branch of the JIAS (Jewish International Aid Society). He was an ultra-Orthodox Jew who could explain the significance of every meaningless ritual proclaimed by some hairsplitting rabbi, but he had no understanding of the essence of Judaism: compassion for your fellow human beings. Going to this man for financial help must have been the hardest thing my father ever did. He made it clear he was not asking for himself.

"I have a growing son who has nothing to eat."

Citrom Yakov looks at him from behind his desk. He has a responsibility not to squander the society's donated funds on able-bodied young men.

"Why don't you work?"

"No one will hire me. The few dollars I get from the bakery go for rent. I can't even afford to buy my son proper footwear."

My father turns to me.

"Show him."

I pull one foot out of my rubber boot to show that I have no socks.

Citrom Yakov pulls his beard thoughtfully. Then he returns to his paperwork.

"There are others worse off than you."

I thought my father was going to hit him. But he just turned around and left, with me trailing after. A few days later, he turned to another pious hypocrite for help.

—

Anton Mihaly, who was married to my mother's sister Giselle, owned a prosperous farm at the foot of the Carpathian Mountains. He was big in grapes and tobacco. Anton and Geezy had several grown sons and daughters all living at home, so my father must have thought they wouldn't notice an extra mouth to feed. And I could help with the harvest.

But my father hadn't spoken to Anton in years, and he wasn't inclined to do so now. He dropped me off a hundred yards from the farm.

"Okay, you can go the rest of the way yourself."

I walk up to the gate and stop.

My father calls to me from the road.

"Go in."

I don't move. I can't impose myself on a man who has no use for me. I'll wait until my uncle invites me in. He must know I'm here. In a small town they spot a newcomer the minute he arrives.

I see someone at the window, behind the curtains.

But no one comes to the door.

My father is getting impatient.

"Go in! Go up and knock on the door!"

I can't do it. I stand there for twenty minutes, hoping my uncle will invite me in, and he stays inside the house, hoping I'll get tired of waiting and go away, while my father yells at me from the road. Finally one of my cousins takes pity on me.

The door opens.

"Come on in."

My uncle made no secret of how he felt about my visit. "How long does your father want you to stay with us?" were the first words out of his mouth.

"I don't know. Can I stay long?"

In spite of the cool reception, I wanted to stay there. Life with my father was miserable.

"We'll see," my aunt Geezy said, watching my uncle out of the corner of her eye.

My aunt was a kind-hearted woman, but a pious Jewish housewife wife did not go against her husband. I arrived the day before *Rosh Hashanah,* so we didn't work for a few days. Instead, we all went to the synagogue. My aunt dressed me up in one of her sons' outfits for the occasion. I looked in the mirror and liked what I saw.

Once again, I didn't feel out of place in the synagogue. I had learned the basic Hebrew prayers in *cheder* and was able to follow along in the prayer book. But then a couple of kids started picking on me and I lost my temper. Right in the middle of the services, I had a fistfight.

My male cousins were proud of me for defending myself, but the rest of the family was shocked. The High Holidays were the holiest period of the Jewish year – a time for prayer and repentance. The small-town congregation was not really surprised by my shocking behaviour. Everyone knew of my situation – I was the son of a non-believer who had dumped me on his in-laws because he couldn't make a living.

My uncle Anton seemed pleased that I had fulfilled his expectations. He expected me to act like a *Goy*, and I did. When the High Holidays ended, seven days later, he was ready to ship me back to the city. But my oldest cousin made him an offer he couldn't refuse.

"Let him stay a couple of extra days. He can help us roll the tobacco."

When tobacco is harvested, the damp leaves are rolled up and stored in a big barn or warehouse to cure. It isn't heavy work, just monotonous. Everyone on the farm, including the women, helped roll the tobacco, and there was a lot of good-natured chatter. Then a stranger walked through the door. Suddenly everything was quite.

The Nylas officer in charge of the district had come to inspect the warehouse. Like the German political police, the Nylas wore not regular uniforms, but black suits with armbands and hobnailed boots. The only difference between them and the Gestapo was that, instead of a swastika, the Nylas officers had a cross-arrow insignia on their armbands. This officer also had grenades in his belt and was drunk. He walked around like he owned the place, making crude jokes and fondling the women.

No one said a thing. We all just sat there silently, hoping he would tire of his little game and walk out.

Finally he did.

This was only one of many disturbing events that took place during my short, relatively happy, stay on my uncle Anton's farm. Another little drama that stands out in my memory is the tragedy of the "unclean" goose.

For months before my arrival, my aunt Geezy had been force-feeding a goose for the High Holidays. Chopped goose liver (the French call it pâté) is a delicacy only rich people and farmers can afford because of all the time and effort involved. The goose is stuffed until it's ready to burst almost from the time it's born. When it's finally slaughtered, its liver is so large a farm family can eat it for weeks.

But a Jewish family can only eat the flesh (or innards) of an animal that has been declared kosher. A few days after my arrival, my aunt took her prize goose to be slaughtered in the prescribed kosher manner.

After the *shoichet* (ritual slaughterer) cut the bird's throat, my aunt took the goose home to prepare it. But when she cut it open to take out the liver, she saw that the intestines had sprung a leak.

"Oy vay, this goose is unclean!"

My aunt was devastated. She had nothing to show for all those months of work – not to mention the expense. She gave the "unclean" goose to a Gentile family. Maybe she got a few dollars for it; I don't remember.

Apart from these little tragedies, life on the farm was pleasant. It was harvest time, and everyone was busy taking in the crops. When I wasn't helping, I played in the backyard. Or took my uncle's animals out to pasture. The weather was mild but not oppressively hot, and the grass was high. After a few hours of watching the animals graze, I'd get bored and bring them back – usually too early, which did not please my uncle. In his eyes I could do nothing right. At the dinner table, he would talk about me as if I wasn't there.

"He's more trouble than he's worth."

That was his favourite expression.

In addition to tobacco, my uncle grew high-quality wine grapes that he sold to a local winery. After the grapes were harvested, we had to get rid of the vines. It was a tricky business because vines are not the easiest things to transport. My uncle would load the wagons so full that we were in danger of losing the entire load every time the wagon hit a rut in the road. My cousins and I walked beside the wagon, trying to keep it steady, but my uncle insisted on riding on top of the vines. A young acrobat would have had trouble staying up there, never mind a middle-aged farmer with a lame leg, but once my uncle got an idea in his head, he could not be talked out of it.

Sure enough, on our first trip, the wagon hit a bump and the stubborn mule lost his balance. Without thinking, I reached out and grabbed him. He was twice my size, but I didn't have time to think, I just acted. Even though I broke my uncle's fall and kept him from breaking an arm or a leg, he didn't thank me. As usual, he saved his comments for the dinner table. "You should have seen the way he jumped," he said in Yiddish. "He thought I was going to fall on top of him!"

Despite my uncle's hostile attitude, life on the farm was better than life in the city with my father. I had enough to eat, my own bed to sleep in, and everyone else in the family treated me like an asset rather than a liability. At harvest time, a farm needs every worker it can get. I felt I was earning my keep, working side by side with my cousins. But one day my uncle made it unmistakably clear how he felt about my contribution to the family. As usual, he made his comments at the dinner table.

"This man is taking the bread out of our mouths."

My aunt started to cry; my cousins just sat there, staring at their plates. Except for my aunt's sniffing, we ate the rest of the meal in silence.

The next morning I went home.

—

My father was not pleased to see me back. "To hell with them," he said when I told him why I had left. After that, he didn't say much of anything. We went back to our routine of living together but apart. I bummed around all day, only coming back to the room to eat a crust of bread and go to sleep beside my father.

But one day I came home and found him in a much better mood. He had prepared a feast – noodles, tomatoes, greens – and it smelled delicious! We had a visitor. He was sitting on an easy chair my father must have dragged in from the living room.

My father's new friend, a retired Hungarian officer, was so fat he couldn't sit on an ordinary kitchen chair. He had just come into town, had heard about my father, and had looked him up. "He wants to open a bakery," my father said.

They discussed the proposition over dinner. The Hungarian, a highly decorated officer, knew nothing about running a bakery, but he would be able to obtain a business licence. There was an empty bakery available, and he had already taken my father to see it. Of course, they couldn't afford to hire any employees. My father would have to do all the work himself.

Running a bakery single-handedly wasn't an easy job, but I knew my dad could do it. When I was younger, he sometimes took me to his bakery. In his heyday, he had two employees to do the heavy work. One of them, Bercu Roth, had taken a liking to me. He was a wonderful man and a hard worker, but he had a bad stutter. He had a close friend with the same speech impediment. I used to laugh to hear the two of them trying to carry on a conversation.

Bercu would laugh too. He never got angry with me. In his eyes I could do no wrong.

Bercu showed me how to prepare the ovens. It was a long and involved process, not just a matter of turning a switch.. You had to chop cords of wood into narrow strips, then lay them across the bottom of the oven in a certain way to distribute the heat evenly.

Then you had to wait for the oven to reach the proper temperature before you put in the dough. If the temperature was too high or too low, or the wood wasn't distributed evenly, it could ruin the baking.

After my father's business went downhill, he did all the work himself. And when he lost the bakery, he had to prepare his bagel dough at home then carry it to the bakery before the ovens cooled off. I remember him getting up at four in the morning, breaking what seemed like hundreds of eggs, and mixing them in huge vats. My dad wasn't afraid of hard work, as long as it was work in which he could take pride.

Over the next few months, he and his "partner" continued to meet. The bakery didn't materialize, but my dad never lost hope. "It's getting closer," he would say. Meanwhile, he had no job and a growing son to feed. He kept trying to find someone who would take me off his hands.

Eventually he sent me to another aunt, one of my mother's sisters, who had a tiny house a few kilometres away in a little town called Marok Papi. She was living with two daughters, one of whom had a bad eye. I don't know if she was a widow. My father never explained anything; I had to figure it out for myself. One thing wasn't very hard to figure out – the last thing this poor woman needed was a non-paying boarder. She didn't have a pot to piss in. Potatoes were the only thing she and her daughters had to eat, and there were not enough of those to share with a young, growing boy. I felt very uncomfortable living with these three women. The older daughter, who had some kind of job in town, was in her late twenties, and the one with the bad eye was a few years older than I was. "Why don't you go out and play with her?" my aunt would say.

So I did. But after three or four days of sharing their potatoes, I went outside by myself – and didn't come back.

—

Once again, my father was not happy to return to our routine together. But one day, a few months later, a well-dressed stranger showed up at our place. He introduced himself to my father, giving a Gentile name, and said, "I work for your brother."

I'd heard my father mention his older half-brother, a man he'd never met who was a big industrialist in Budapest. According to rumours, this half-brother had changed his name to Wandor (which means "wanderer" in Hungarian) and married a Christian woman. The stranger said he was an executive of a big company run by my father's half-brother.

"He knew I was going through Beregszasz and told me to look you up. But he didn't think I'd find you."

My father didn't believe this story – he thought this man *was* his half-brother but had assumed a false identity to spare my father embarrassment. We were not exactly living in luxury. "I'd invite you in for a cup of coffee," my father said, "but I'm afraid I don't have any."

"That's all right," the man replied. "Let me invite you to a restaurant."

It was an offer my father couldn't refuse.

At the restaurant, the well-dressed stranger bought us a nice dinner and confirmed the rumours we'd heard. My father's half-brother was head of a company that produced vacuum-sealed cans of food. He had twelve hundred employees. Just before he left, this "employee" took out a notepad, wrote something on it, and handed the note to my father.

"You can reach your brother at this address."

Over the next few days, my father read the name and address on that scrap of paper a thousand times. He couldn't stop talking about the mysterious visitor. He was sure the man was not an executive of his half-brother's company but Wandor himself.

Finally my father wrote a letter to his half-brother to show that he was in on the joke:

Dear Sir,

It was nice of you to send this man to see me. I'm sure he told you that my situation is not too good, that I have a growing son I can't afford to feed. If it is not too much to ask, would you mind if I sent him to stay with you for awhile?

—

The man who met me at the train station was well dressed, but that was his only resemblance to the stranger who had come to visit us. My father's half-brother was a short middle-aged man with a neatly trimmed moustache and a twinkle in his eye. "I'm your uncle," he said and introduced himself as Wandor something – I don't remember his first name.

His wife, a nice-looking woman, gave me a big hug when I walked through the door. Apparently my uncle *had* adopted his wife's religion. There was nothing "Jewish" about their apartment, yet I immediately felt more at home in this Gentile house than I had living with my Orthodox uncles.

"This is where you'll sleep," my aunt said, taking me to an airy bedroom that had a special kid's bed with drawers under it. When I climbed into bed that first night, I thought I was in heaven. The quilt was soft as a cloud and the sheets felt like silk. To wet such bedclothes would be terrible. Before I fell asleep, I asked God to please wake me up if I had to go during the night.

It didn't help.

I covered up the wet spot, hoping my aunt wouldn't notice, but later that morning she took off all the bedding, took everything out of the drawers, opened the window, and remade the bed with a plastic sheet. I kept waiting for her to scold me – after all, I was a big boy – but she didn't say anything.

A few days later, while we were eating, my uncle made a joke.

"Did you know your father was a bedwetter?"

I couldn't believe my ears.

My uncle reassured me.

"You grow out of it."

When? I felt like asking. I was already past the age when a Jewish boy was supposed to become a man. Of course, I was immature for my age. My kindersheh shtick (childish ways) had been a constant complaint of my stepmother – and an ongoing source of irritation to my father – but this couple, whose own children were already grown, seemed to enjoy having me around. They took particular delight in showing this thirteen-year-old bumpkin the wonders of the big city.

Modern Budapest was made up of two old cities – Buda and Pest – that were separated by the Danube River. The *Duna*, as it is called in Europe, isn't blue, but it was a beautiful, wide river with ferry boats going back and forth, from one side to the other.

I was dying to ride them, and, thanks to my uncle, I had the chance. "We're going to the zoo today," he said to me at breakfast one morning. "You'd better get ready for the trip."

It wasn't much of a trip, just across the river, but I can remember it like it was yesterday. You bought a token at a little window and when you got on the boat, you dropped the token into a narrow slot. The box had a glass window so you could see the token after you'd dropped it in. At the zoo you bought a ticket at another window and when you went through the gate, a man tore it in half and gave you the stub.

We walked around for hours looking at the strange and exotic animals while I stuffed myself with popcorn, cotton candy, and all kinds of junk. It was a beautiful, sunny day and, for one of the few times in my life, I was perfectly relaxed and happy. But as we headed for the exit, a cloud appeared on the horizon. My uncle asked if I had my ticket stub.

"No, I threw it away. Why?"

He shook his head.

"They won't let you out without your ticket stub."

Suddenly I got worried.

"Where am I going to sleep?"

My aunt laughed.

"The same place you slept last night. He's just teasing you."

My uncle laughed.

I laughed too.

I laughed more during the short time I spent with these lovely people than I had in my entire life. I wish my mother's siblings were as nice. This Christian couple, who had never laid eyes on me before I stepped off the train, treated me like a long-lost son.

After about ten days, my uncle put me back on the train for home.

And that was the end of the laughter.

The Eliases, adoptive parents

Employment

I was home but no longer walking the streets. After three years of looking, my father had finally found work. Not in a bakery but in a barrel factory. Reisman's was a well-established business that had been making wine barrels for centuries. Now they were making wooden barrels to ship munitions. The war was going badly for Germany, and Hitler needed all the factories he could get. Since I had nothing better to do, I used to go to work with my father and watch the men make barrels.

I thought barrel making was beautiful – a simple yet very precise process that took a bit of strength and a great deal of skill. You took a number of flat pieces of wood (staves) of different sizes and lined them up, side by side vertically, inside an iron ring. Then you had to place another ring around the top and hit it with a hammer until the staves began to bend. Then you turned the wood over and knocked down the other ring a few inches. You continued this process until the loose staves were squeezed together into the shape of a waterproof barrel. Your only tools were two hammers, one with a notch that held the ring in place as you hit it with the other hammer. The whole operation was carried out over a basket of burning coals in order to keep the metal rings from contracting. If they cooled off too soon, one of the staves might break and the barrel would be ruined.

I came to the factory so often that one of the barrel makers took me on as a helper. He paid me a few pennies and showed me what to do. Pretty soon I could make barrels better than he could. The other men sometimes stood around to watch me. Even Mr. Reisman would stop by to take a look. He couldn't get over it – a young boy was doing a job that grown men couldn't handle. Working in the barrel factory, I got stronger and more confident every day. I felt like I was finally beginning to grow up.

The only thing that didn't grow was my salary. I was working like a horse and earning chicken feed. But I loved it.

My dad, who worked on one of the machines, hated it. He wanted to be a baker. After a few months at the barrel factory, he got his wish.

—

Within a few months, my father's new bakery was doing enough business for him to hire a worker. At first, my dad had done everything himself. The Hungarian officer would come down and watch. He'd sit on his fat ass, smoking cigarettes and drinking coffee, while his "partner" worked like an ox. The first bread came out beautiful. Eventually, in addition to a helper, my dad got a kneading machine.

Since I continued to work at Reisman's, we hardly ever saw each other. I worked all day and slept like a log at night. My dad worked at night and slept during the day. When I wasn't making barrels, I was bumming around the streets. The only time I saw my father was on the one day a week when the ovens were allowed to cool. I don't remember if it was a Saturday or a Sunday. I just remember that on one of those days off he suggested something that hit me like a barrel hammer.

"Let's go visit your sister."

"Who?"

"Your sister, Szidi."

"Szidi? Szidi...."

I was so overwhelmed at the idea of seeing my sister again that I kept repeating her name over and over all the way there. The people who had adopted her, Dezso and Hanna Elias, lived in Fehkete Ardo, a small town a few hours away by train. After we got off

Szidi, my sister

the train, we had to walk another ten kilometres to the Elias's house. They were expecting us.

"Come in, come in," they said, meeting us at the door. They seemed like very nice people and couldn't say enough about Szidi. "She's a very good girl," they kept saying. "We're very happy with her."

I wondered where she was.

"She's outside playing."

"Can I go call her in?"

"Sure, go ahead."

Just as I come out of the house, a young girl walks through the gate. I look at her, and it's like looking in a mirror.

She stops and looks at me.

"You're my brother."

I nod. I'm too emotional to speak.

For a few seconds we just stand there, looking at each other. My sister was a baby the last time I saw her yet I feel I've known this pretty young girl all my life. It's love at first sight. Eventually, I find my voice.

"Let's go inside."

We walk in. My father gets up and hugs and kisses her. She hugs him back, like he's really her father instead of a strange man whom she wouldn't even recognize if she passed him on the street. I was the older brother, but Szidi has much more *chaine*. "This is my mother and father," she says, introducing me to the Eliases. Then she sits down beside me.

They had been talking about the bedwetting problem. The Eliases said that Szidi hadn't wet the bed since she was five years old.

Mrs. Elias gives my father the remedy.

"You have to keep them warm."

A woman showed her how to make a special poultice that you heated up on the stove. Every night, for two months, she tied it around Szidi's waist when she went to sleep.

Mrs. Elias smiles.

"And it cleared up the problem."

My father nods – he's listening with half an ear.

To me, it's a revelation. I didn't know there was a remedy for my condition. No one would have gone to that much trouble for me, but I was thrilled that Szidi had ended up with such thoughtful people. Later in the day, we went out for a walk and I couldn't stop looking at her.

"Are you really my sister?"

She shrugs.

"I don't know."

I ask her a million questions.

She doesn't know any of the answers.

We meet one of her girlfriends.

"This is my brother."

The girl looks at me and laughs.

"You have the same face."

To me it's a compliment because my sister is so beautiful.

—

It was such a good feeling to be with Szidi that I didn't want to leave. It would be heaven to live with nice people in a house with a big yard, two cows, and a horse and buggy. The Eliases had invited us to sleep over so maybe they would agree to let me stay. Maybe that's why my father had brought me, hoping they would take me off his hands.

That night, when my father goes for a walk, I tell the Eliases about my stepmother and how my father can't cope with me. They are very sympathetic, but they don't offer to adopt me. They are no longer a young couple. They have their own troubles.

The next morning I kiss my sister goodbye.

I will never see her again.

DEPORTATION

Our days in Beregszasz were numbered. Shortly after we returned from seeing my sister, my father and I were shipped to Auschwitz. I'm not too clear on the sequence of events because everything happened so quickly – bang! bang! bang! It was the late spring of 1944, and the "invincible" German war machine had shifted into reverse. The only thing that was going ahead full speed was the "Final Solution." Through trial and error, the Nazi butchers had learned to carry out Hitler's insane plan with increasing efficiency. Under German supervision, Hungary was able to make herself *Judenrein* (clean of Jews) in record time. The whole operation took a matter of weeks.

In Warsaw, the military had built a wall around a section of the city; in Beregszasz, they simply turned factory complexes into ghettos. My father and I ended up in an unused brick factory with hundreds of other families. There was a high fence around the factory, and you had to go in and out through a main gate, where a guard checked your pass. If you had a job, you were given a day pass. My father continued to work at the bakery, and I seem to remember going to work too. But I couldn't have gone for very long because Reisman's was also turned into a ghetto.

Living in the ghetto wasn't comfortable, but it was bearable. You had a place to sleep, a place to eat, and if you wanted privacy, you hung up a blanket. Several times a day, a soldier came into the building to make sure everyone was there. He called out the names from a list, and if a family member was missing, you had to explain why:

"My father's at work ... my mother's in the hospital ..."

If no one offered an explanation, the soldier waited a few hours for the missing people to show up, then went looking for them with guns. Surprisingly, they didn't have to go looking very often.

The fence wasn't barbed wire, just an ordinary factory fence that wasn't much of a barrier to a fit young man. All a person had to do was wait until no guards were around, climb over the fence and run into the forest, but people didn't want to leave their families. Even under these difficult conditions, we tried to go on with our lives. Had we known what lay in store for us, here, there would have been far more attempts to escape.

I had no idea what was going on and, as usual, my father didn't explain anything. I doubt that he knew himself. The guards kept telling us not to worry; we were just being housed in the ghetto prior to "resettlement." They deliberately kept us in the dark. If you want people to climb into a cattle car, you give them something to hang on to – even if it's only an illusion.

Illusions were all that the Jews of Hungary had left. We had been ordered to turn in all our money and jewellery. Machine guns were set up in the ghetto and people were stopped and searched. One day, I witnessed a scene I will never forget.

Our former landlady is out walking with her daughters. Two Hungarian soldiers stop her and tell her to open her purse. She hesitates. One of the soldiers grabs the purse out of her hands, opens it, and pulls out a few bills.

"What's this?" he says, sticking them in her face.

The poor woman stands there, tongue-tied.

The soldiers grab her, one on each arm, and stand her up against the wall.

Her daughters start screaming.

One of the soldiers points a machine gun at her and gets ready to fire.

The woman faints.

The soldiers walk away.

It was indescribable – like the Stone Age. They left this woman, who had hidden a few dollars to support her two daughters, lying on the ground like so much trash. It wasn't necessary to shoot her – they had made their point. When the authorities told you to do something, you did it. After that, whenever I saw money sticking out of cracks in the ghetto wall, where people had hidden it, I was never tempted to take it.

—

After a few weeks, the deportation began, starting with the Jews in the outlying ghettos. I would see them being trucked into the city. Young men, old men, women, children, babies – I'd watch them being loaded onto cattle cars and wonder what would become of them. I'd heard a few people in the ghetto talking about *Auschwitz*, but the word meant nothing to me.

Eventually the soldiers got around to our ghetto. One soldier stood on the back of a truck and shouted out the names.

One day, as I'm watching them load the train, I hear the name of my father's cousin – the one who helped stop my nosebleed – Ignac Weissberger. As he walks into the boxcar, the soldier calling out the names makes a joke out of my uncle's name. "Ignac *Engem Tobet Nem Latc* (You'll Never See Me Again)," he calls out and laughs.

It sends a shiver down my back.

—

My father and I were among the last to be shipped out. Boarding the train wasn't so bad; it was pushing the old ladies ahead of me that I found painful. We were loaded onto a cattle car with two small, barred windows, high on either side. The soldiers jammed sixty or seventy of us into the car, slammed the door shut, and locked it from the outside.

It would not be opened again until we reached our destination.

—

The six-day train ride was a nightmare. You couldn't breathe – there wasn't enough air – and there was no room to sit down. If you wanted to sleep, you had to lean against the wall or a neighbour. I stood all the way. But I had young legs. My dad took some food – a bread sandwich or something – but it ran out in the first few days. I don't remember what I ate – for once in my life I didn't care about food. Hunger was nothing compared to the endless torture of that journey.

Old people are falling down, crying, crawling around on their hands and knees, looking for a place to lie down. During the day, the sun beats down and the car grows as hot as an oven. People are lying on the floor, unconscious. The few cans of water we were given have run out days ago. When the train stops, one of the younger men climbs up to the small window and yells for water.

Nobody pays attention.

We bang on the door.

The guards shoot off rifles.

So we stop banging.

Day after day this went on. Where were we going? How long would it take to get there? Whenever the train stopped, one of the younger men would climb up on a suitcase or a box, look out the window, and tell us what he could see.

Usually it wasn't much.

Then one day the guy at the window saw something worth mentioning.

"Die Deuchen zeinen do (The Germans are here)."

—

I climb up on a suitcase and look out the narrow window. I see a train yard with a bunch of men. A few of them are wearing military uniforms and piss pot helmets and carrying rifles. They look well-fed, but most of the other people I see are wearing loose-fitting suits with wide blue and white stripes. They look like human scarecrows. As the scarecrows shuffle around in their wooden clogs, train doors are slamming and orders are being shouted:

"Raus! Raus! Mach shnell! (Out! Out! Hurry up!)"

Standing off to the side, observing, is an officer in a smart black uniform, shiny boots, leather gloves, and a cap with a short peak. On the front of the cap I see a skull and crossbones and on his lapels is a strange insignia that looks like two lighting bolts. This is the first time I've seen those fancy esses that I will learn to despise.

As I get down from the window, an older man climbs up, looks out, and makes an announcement in Yiddish.

"Mir zeinen in Auschwitz (We're in Auschwitz)."

The journey was over but the nightmare continued. They unloaded the train one car at a time, and it was a long train – maybe sixty or seventy cars. Our car was near the end. The waiting was torture. I didn't care what was waiting for me – I just wanted to smell fresh air and move my limbs. We stood in the train yard for a full day with the door locked. Then finally the door rolled open with a bang.

I walk out of the car, blinded by sunlight.

I look over my shoulder for my dad and see people lying on the floor of the car, not moving. Some of the men in striped uniforms are pulling at them, trying to get them to their feet.

The Heftlings (inmates) did all the work in the camps; the SS merely supervised. That was the Nazi way– make the victim dig his own grave. Occasionally, an ordinary soldier might get his boots dirty, but the SS officers just strutted around in their fancy uniforms like black peacocks. Even among the Heftlings there was a pecking order. Those with a skill or a trade might sew uniforms, cut hair, or keep records, but supervisory positions – like Block Eldster (block leader), Kapo (head man) and Camp Eldster (camp leader) were reserved for "higher" types, like political prisoners. The Heftlings unloading the train were near the bottom of the pecking order. They were Jews.

"Try and walk," I hear one say, in Yiddish, to an old man he has managed to pull to his feet. The old man manages to takes a few shaky steps. Not everyone on the floor is capable of standing, let alone walking. A few are no longer breathing. Some of my fellow passengers walk off the train, some are dragged, others are carried.

We are marched in a line toward an SS officer who is standing between two armed guards, directing traffic.

"To the left, to the right, to the left...."

It would be years before I learned this man's name: Joseph Mengele. If I bumped into him on the street, I wouldn't know him. He was just an ordinary-looking German who had usurped the power of the Almighty. With a wave of his hand, "Dr. Mengele" decided who would live and who would die.

As my father and I approach the front of the line, I see Mengele directing the river of Jews into two streams, like Moses parting the Red Sea. He is separating the old from the young, the weak from the strong, husbands from wives, parents from children....

"Zug as do bist aichtsen (Say you're eighteen)," a Heftling whispers in my ear.

No one asks me. I stand on tiptoe so I look the same height as my father.

When we reach the front of the line, I don't even look at Mengele, just follow my father. I'm smaller than a kid in front of me who was separated from his father, but no one comes after me, so I keep walking.

Why didn't Mengele stop me? I don't know. Maybe it was because we were among the last ones off the train. After a long day, the Nazi Moses couldn't be bothered to interrupt the flow of the river for the sake of one little fish. In that way, I slipped through the net.

The guards march us to a building that looks like a big barn with a wide door.

One of them points with his rifle.

"Inside."

I follow my father through the door.

Just inside the entrance I see two huge piles: one of clothes, one of eyeglasses.

It's a shocking sight.

"Take off your clothes."

Everyone began to undress, but I was reluctant to expose myself to strangers. At home I wouldn't even undress in front of my father. I was a late bloomer. If there was a doubt about my being a "man," my genitals would resolve it. So I appealed to the guard.

"What about my shoes and pants? I need them."

"Don't worry about it. You'll get nice clothes."

So I did as I was told.

Pretty soon we were all standing there naked – our clothes and eyeglasses now part of the piles.

"Walk that way," the guard says, pointing with his rifle.

We walked to an area where other newcomers were getting haircuts. The barbers – also Heftlings – were fast but not gentle. And they weren't just cutting hair; they were shaving heads, armpits, and pubic areas with dry razors, leaving a few cuts and scratches.

Finally it's my turn.

The barber looks at the peach fuzz on my genital area and makes a face.

"Do we have to shave you too?"

Everyone laughs.

Even my father smiles and makes a joke.

"I didn't even know you had hair down there."

I was both embarrassed and pleased by this attention. Although I hated to be the butt of a joke, I was glad to give everyone something to laugh about. The workers shaved off my few hairs and I followed my father to another room, where we took a shower. It was a special shower with some kind of disinfectant that burned my skin. Then we had to submerge ourselves in a tub of even stronger disinfectant – the kind they use on animals.

It's a big tub with a step leading up to it. We go in two at a time.

I slip on the step and fall in, head first.

It feels like I'm being skinned alive.

My eyes and nostrils burn like hell.

As we emerge from the tub a Heftling is waiting with a pump gun.

He sprays us from head to toe with a white powder.

"Go take a shower."

We walk back into the shower room, looking like ghosts.

We showered again; then went to get our clothing.

I am lined up, naked, behind other naked men who are moving past a long table where a Heftling is handing out bundles of clothing.

"Nem doos (Take this)," he says, handing one to me.

I open the pile and look at my uniform: a jacket, pants, and cap – all in the same faded blue-and-white-striped cloth I saw on the Heftlings who had unloaded the train.

"Can I put it on?"

"Yeah."

I get dressed. It's a relief to have my body covered again. My new clothes are loose and rough, but I don't mind. I put on my wooden clogs and march outside for a ritual that will be repeated over and over, every morning, noon, and night, for months to come – my first Tzail Appel (counting parade).

The Nazis were meticulous record keepers. After the liberation, the Allies found stacks and stacks of paper on which soldiers had recorded every confiscated item. The camps were run with the same efficiency that the Germans applied to any other enterprise. Guards lined us up in rows of five so that the SS officer who conducted the Tzail Appel could tell at once if anyone was missing – he just had to count the rows and multiply by two – ten, twenty, thirty, forty....

After the officer finished the count, the guards marched us single file to a table where one Heftling was recording names and another was tattooing forearms.

It was a slow process.

I am standing there for what seems like hours when suddenly a truck drives up and soldiers. jump off the back. They come over and walk up and down, pulling kids out of the line.

"Get in the truck."

I watch six or seven kids from my hometown climb onto the back of the truck.

The ones who don't move fast enough are shoved forward with the barrel of a rifle.

Then someone grabs my arm.

A soldier is dragging me and another kid toward the truck.

I tear myself away and start running.

I hear the soldier shouting.

"Stop! Stop or I'll shoot!"

I keep running. If he shoots me, he shoots me – I'm going to die anyway.

The soldier doesn't shoot; he comes after me.

I kick off my clogs and dodge in and out among the Heftlings.

The soldier can't catch me.

The ground is sandy and he keeps slipping.

I hear him yelling and swearing at me.

Every time I come through a break in the line, I see my dad watching me.

He has a terrible look on his face.

Then I hear the soldier on the truck yell something that makes my heart leap.

"Forget him, we're ready to go!"

Suddenly no one was chasing me. The soldier was back on the truck. I watched it pull away with its cargo of kids my age. Then I collected my clogs, put them on, and rejoined my father. He tried to smile at me but had trouble.

—

The tattoo artist is a Polish Jew and the Heftling recording the names is a German Jew.

"Nomen (Name)?"

"Weisz, Erno."

He makes a face.

"Erno is kein nomen (Erno is not a name)."

He translates it into German.

"Weisz, Ernst."

He writes down my new name beside a number and I move down the line to the tattoo artist.

"Roll up your sleeve."

I roll it up.

The needle hurts like hell, but it only takes a few minutes.

"Next."

My arm continued to bleed for a while, but that was a small price to pay for a new lease on life. You don't brand an animal you are going to slaughter. Years later my tattoo would become a painful reminder, but at the time it was a great relief. I was perfectly happy to trade my identity as Weisz, Erno, gas chamber candidate, for Weisz, Ernst, slave labourer A-9654. My father was A-9655.

BEAST OF BURDEN

In September 1939, immediately after they invaded Poland, the Germans began to build a *Farnichtenlager* (death camp) at Auschwitz-Birkenau, which is located about sixty kilometres west of Krakow, in eastern Upper Silesia. The original camp was a solidly built complex of brick buildings that housed offices, examination rooms, staff quarters, and row upon row of sleeping blocks sufficient for ten thousand Heftlings (inmates).

But even this facility proved too small and inefficient to carry out Hitler's plan of exterminating every Jew in Europe by the end of 1942. The overworked crematorium constantly broke down, and there was not enough manpower or land to bury the bodies that kept piling up. In March of 1941, the Nazi efficiency experts built a new extermination camp with more up-to-date crematoria and fewer "luxuries," three kilometres away. By the time my father and I arrived, toward the end of 1944, the new camp was also too small and inefficient to handle the load.

Birkenau was the camp at which all new arrivals were unloaded from cattle cars. Unlike Auschwitz proper, it was a large compound of flimsy one-storey buildings that blended so well into the surrounding forest that it couldn't be seen from the air. If not for the railway tracks leading up to the gate, you wouldn't know it was there. And if not for the high barbed wire fence, you might think it was a summer camp.

Deception was the rule at Auschwitz-Birkenau. The Nazi efficiency experts knew that Hitler's killing machine would run more smoothly if victims were kept in the dark. The SS had learned its trade from the master of deception:

The magnitude of a lie always contains a certain factor of credibility, since the great masses of the people ... more easily fall victim to a big lie than a little one.

On the way to the gas chamber, naked prisoners would be handed bars of soap to create the illusion that they were going to have a shower. When the Sonderkommando (the Heftlings with the dirtiest jobs) aired out the "shower room," they would collect the soap – made from human fat – so that it could be handed to the next group.

During my short stay at Birkenau, I didn't even see a gas chamber or any of the three crematoria. We were confined in an entirely different section of the camp until it was time to ship us out to a slave labour camp.

But, as they marched us down the road to Auschwitz, there was a sickeningly sweet smell in the air.

I look around to see where it's coming from.

I see black smoke rising from a clearing in the forest.

"What's that?" I ask my father.

He doesn't answer – just keeps walking with his eyes straight ahead.

Later, I discovered what the smell was. There was a bottleneck at the crematoria, so they were burning bodies in open pits, using human fat as fuel. The Sonderkommando were ordered to dig huge trenches with depressions at either end to catch the melting fat. When the trench was full, they poured kerosene over the bodies to start the fire, then shovelled the liquid fat back over the bodies to keep it going. Slave labour was no picnic, but being a Sonderkommando was unimaginable.

At the entrance to Auschwitz, we passed through an iron gate that said *Arbeit Macht Frei* (Work Makes You Free). I wondered if it was true. The camp was older than Birkenau but not as shabby. The SS ran the show and they liked everything spic and span. The blocks weren't wooden huts but brick buildings, and each block had an *Eldster* (leader) who was responsible for keeping the place clean.

As soon as we arrived, we had a *Tzail Appel* and were assigned to a block. There were about sixty people in my block. After we had been assigned bunks – I took an upper so my father, who was too weak to climb, could have a lower – there was another *Tzail Appel* and then the *Block Eldster* made a short speech.

"In a few days you will be shipped out to another camp for arbeit (work). In the meantime, you can go out and walk around. But don't wander away. If you don't answer when your name is called, you will be severely punished."

For several days, all we did was eat, sleep, and wait. They fed us three times a day, but gave us so little food that I was always hungry. Still, compared to Birkenau, this was a vacation camp. We weren't all Jews; there were other "inferior" races, as well as political prisoners, war prisoners, and ordinary criminals. There were all kinds of activities for the amusement of the SS, and sometimes the Heftlings were allowed to watch. I remember seeing a boxing match between a tall French war prisoner and a short, stocky Polish convict. The SS had put up a ring in the middle of the camp for the fight. The Frenchman had a longer reach and was a better boxer, but the Polish guy came in from underneath and was winning the fight. The crowd, who were mostly Polish Jews, was cheering for the Pole. "Knock him out, knock him out!" they all yelled.

Finally they got their wish – the Frenchman hit the canvas.

A cheer went up from the crowd.

I cheered as loudly as the others. That was my first boxing match and I've been a fan ever since. For a short time, those two men in the ring made me forget where I was. About a week later, the *Block Eldster* reminded us.

"Okay, it's time to go."

A truck was already waiting in front of the block.

"You're going to Yavoszno," the truck driver said under his breath as we climbed onto the back. (Ordinarily, they didn't tell you a thing, so he had to be careful.) "It takes about half an hour," he whispered. Then he put the truck in gear and, as the sun began to sink, drove us out the gate that said "Work Makes You Free."

—

Yavoszno was a campsite of prefabricated wooden buildings and not much else. When we arrived just before sunset, they were still putting up the building that was to be our block. We waited for them to finish after we were unloaded from the truck, but it didn't take long to put up four walls and a roof. As soon as the workers left, the guards marched us inside. There were three tiers of bunks, with just enough room between them to squeeze a body. Each bunk was just a wooden box with a straw mattress, but within a few days I was so exhausted at the end of the day I could have slept on a rock.

Once we were in our bunks, the *Block Eldster* locked the door and it stayed locked until it was time to get up for *arbeit*. If you had to urinate during the night, you went in a little pail. In the morning you emptied your pail into a big metal barrel with two handles that stood by the door, and two Heftlings would carry the barrel outside and dump it somewhere. The barrel had a cover so the smell of urine inside the block wasn't too bad. There was never anything but urine to dump because no one ever moved his bowels at night. Or even much during the day. There was nothing to move.

This was our daily routine: Morning came and a whistle sounded. We slept in our clothes so it took only a few minutes for everyone to dump his pail and line up outside for *Tzail Appel* by the SS guards. After the head count, wagons rolled up with three or four vats of coffee. The coffee containers were huge urns with a sort of spring-loaded lid and two handles on the side. That was breakfast. The urns were taken off the wagon and we lined up with our cups.

Everyone carried his own eating utensils – a spoon, an aluminum plate, and a cup. Some Heftlings used an old tomato can instead of a cup. One cup of coffee was what you went to work on, so you wanted your container to hold as much as possible. And you wanted to get as close as possible to the front of the line so that the coffee would still be hot.

Whenever I came outside, I always looked for my father. I was more worried about him than about myself. He was no longer the father I used to know– all the life had gone out of him. When I think back, I can hardly believe he was only forty-four. To me, he was an old man.

One morning I saw him standing near the front of the line – with his shaved head, stooped shoulders, and sunken cheeks – when a couple of Polish guys shoved him aside and got in line in front of him.

I go crazy.

These two Heftlings don't know what hit them.

Within minutes, they are lying on the ground, bleeding.

If I'd had time to think, I might not have acted so impulsively. After all, there were SS men standing just a few feet away, watching. But rather than punishing me, they congratulated me on my "victory." Our German jailers loved to see Heftlings at each other's throats. We couldn't talk to each other without permission, but we could beat each other to death and the SS would stand around and watch, smiling. I had put on a show for them. It was even better than the fight between the Frenchman and the Pole because I was even more of an underdog. It wasn't every day that you saw a fourteen-year-old beat the hell out of two adult Heftlings, but because my father couldn't defend himself, I felt I had no choice, just as my father had had no choice when someone had bloodied my nose in *cheder*: Our roles had been reversed. It wasn't until my father defended me that I realized he had some feeling for me. And he was equally surprised by my attack on the two Poles. Later, he would say to me, with tears in his eyes, "I didn't know you loved me."

Once we had our coffee, we would line up for another *Tzail Appel*. If no one was missing, we were split into groups of fifty and marched to the work site, a munitions plant, about five kilometres down the road.

On the way to the munitions plant, we marched past a prisoner of war camp, where British officers would sometimes be outside, playing volleyball. They always stopped to watch us, the way you watch a parade.

Did they know who we were?

I have no way of knowing.

The munitions plant was like a village, with streets, buildings, and train tracks that came right up to loading docks. A high fence surrounded the entire factory complex. I couldn't tell whether the fence was electrified, but there were civilian workers at the plant, so it probably wasn't.

Once we are inside the gate, our German escort does another Tzail Appel.

We are all here.

"Dismissed."

We all go to our jobs.

Each group worked in a different location. My group unloaded bricks from a train. It was backbreaking work because we were bending all the time. One guy pushed the bricks over the edge of the car, so we could get a grip, then we each picked up an armload and carried the bricks to a loading platform. This went on all day. We unloaded one car, then another – by the end of the first day I could hardly straighten up. Next morning, the routine was the same. This became my daily job for the first four months. If it wasn't bricks, it was two-by-fours; if it wasn't from a flatcar, it was from a boxcar – we were always unloading something. To this day, I have chronic back pain.

In the middle of the day, we stopped for half an hour to eat.

Wagons roll up with vats of soup and a huge ladle.

We all line up with our tomato cans.

No one rushes to get to the front of the line – all the "good stuff" is at the bottom.

If the guy with the ladle was a mensch, he would occasionally stir the soup so that some of the vegetables (there was never any meat) might float to the surface. But most of them couldn't be bothered, so after breaking our backs all morning, most of us got a can of hot water to sustain us for the rest of the day. If you were lucky, the hot water might contain a piece of carrot or potato. Some days I was lucky; some days not.

At six o'clock the whistle blows.

I look for my father and line up beside him.

Another count.

Then we march back to camp.

For dinner we get a portion of bread.

It's dark, hard German bread and I hate it.

But it stops the hunger pangs for a while.

The soldiers would cut the loaves in half or in three pieces, depending on orders that came down from the top: Supplies are low, cut down! As we marched in from work, a kid whom the officers used as a runner would stand at the gate and hold up two or three fingers. We didn't have to look at his fingers, just his face. If he had a big smile, it meant we would be going to bed with our shrunken stomachs relatively full. Usually, I went to bed hungry.

With the bread, we either got a piece of cheese or something else. The cheese smelled to high heaven, and some people couldn't stomach it so they went around trading: a piece of cheese for a piece of bread. But I loved the cheese. One day we got a slice of liverwurst. I can still taste it!

In spite of my hunger, I never ate my portion of bread at one sitting; I always saved something for later. If I woke up in the middle of the night to relieve myself, I couldn't fall back to sleep unless I had something to kill the hunger pangs. So I'd eat half my daily ration of bread and put the other half under my pillow. If I slept through the night, I'd have something to eat with my morning coffee.

One morning, after we'd been in camp for a few months, I woke up to find part of my bread missing. I go crazy.

"Someone stole half my bread! Someone stole half my bread!"

I make such a fuss that the Block Eldster comes over to talk to me.

The Germans are very strict about taking anybody else's food.

If I don't calm down, there will be hell to pay.

"What do you mean half?" the Block Eldster says, trying to convince me that I'm imagining things. "If I wanted to steal your bread, do you think I'd leave half under your pillow?"

"Maybe you would. How do I know what a thief would do?"

There was no way I could have been wrong about the missing bread. When all you have to eat is one small portion of bread, you know if a crumb is missing. And if it is, you get down on your hands and knees and look for it. I wouldn't shut up about the theft.

While we are drinking our coffee, I am still making a fuss.

An older man from the block approaches me.

He puts his hand on my arm and lowers his voice.

"Mein kind, du vilst vissen? Dein tatte hot ztuggenem a shtickle broit. (My child, do you want to know? Your father took a piece of bread)."

I look at him like he's crazy. Why would my father steal my bread? All he has to do is ask and I'd share it with him.

I thought the man was lying just to calm me down – and it worked. By the time we lined up for *Tzail Appel,* I had cooled off. Now I realize that he was probably telling the truth. The *Block Eldster* was right: any *Heftling* other than my father would have stolen *all* my bread.

Concern for one's neighbour was a luxury we couldn't afford. If you worried about anyone but yourself, you'd go out of your mind. You didn't make friends with the guy in the next bunk because he might be dead in the morning. People around me were dying every day. All of us were skin and bones. We weren't human beings; we were the walking dead. I didn't think about the future; I just thought about food. Getting a slightly larger piece of bread at the end of the day meant the difference between happiness and sorrow.

I've heard fellow survivors tell about brutal guards who beat Heftlings to death. If I saw any of that, I don't remember it. And I'm not willing to dig for those memories. I closed my eyes and ears to what was going on around me in order to retain my sanity.

But even in hell there are a few kind souls. Hundreds of Polish civilians worked at the munitions plant, and some of them took pity on us. Seeing these walking corpses arrive for work every morning must have been hard on the women who worked in the kitchen because they sometimes left table scraps for us. When we arrived in the morning, we sometimes saw a greasy paper bag sitting on the sidewalk. We couldn't touch it until after *Tzail Appel*, but whoever ran fast enough could get to it before anyone else. I was a fast runner.

There was another fast runner, a Polish kid about my age, and we made a deal: whoever got to the bag first would share it with the other. Usually, we only shared some rotten fruit or potato peelings, but once in a while we got a bone with a little chicken still on it. Then he hurt his leg and couldn't run any more. I kept up my end of the bargain. It could just as easily have been me who had hurt his leg at work. But even though I continued to share the bag with him, I could tell that he thought I was taking advantage of his injury. He would limp up, I would hand him his share, and he would give me a look like the uncle who thought I was stealing the food from his mouth.

One morning, when the bag didn't contain much that was edible, he confronted me.

"What's this?" he says, when I hand him his share.

"That's all there was."

"You're lying. You ate the good stuff before I got here!"

That was the end of our sharing – and our friendship.

Although we had almost nothing to eat, there was no shortage of water. At the camp there was a tap with a hose attached to it, and we just went over and helped ourselves. Someone told me that if you drank enough water ,you would get diarrhoea and have to go to the hospital for a day instead of to work. I drank and drank but finally gave up when I remained constipated. Loading bricks all day, bloated with water, was worse than working on an empty stomach.

Usually, we worked from sunup to sundown, but one day we were given a few hours off. When we went outside for our morning *Tzail Appel,* there was a terrible hubbub. SS men were running around all over the place. It turned out the *Camp Eldster*, a German political prisoner, had escaped. Soldiers with rifles and tracking dogs went looking for him, but they never found him. The man the SS had entrusted with such a privileged position had simply walked away from the camp and disappeared into the crowd. This wasn't such a great trick in a country that was crawling with

Germans. The SS had trusted the wrong man – they should have made a Jew *Camp Eldster.*

The only exceptional thing about this incident is that it meant we went to work a few hours late. The people in charge of us were always coming and going. You never knew from one day to the next who would be giving you orders; you just knew that when they said jump, you'd better jump, especially if the order came from the SS. The young SS officers were the worst – they had to prove how tough they were.

But even among the SS there were a few human beings. One older officer had a soft spot for young people. Maybe he had children of his own. Shortly after he arrived, he was walking around the munitions plant when he saw a bunch of us kids unloading bricks.

"This is no job for you," he said to us. "I'll find something else for you to do. Maybe you'll learn a trade here."

I didn't know if he was kidding us or himself, but about a week later he showed up again and picked out each of the younger guys on the loading crew.

"You, come with me."

We stopped working and lined up, about sixteen of us.

"Follow me."

We followed him to a foundry.

"Here we make different things from iron. You can learn this."

He let us walk around. It was like being back in the barrel factory – I felt right at home.

A worker was holding a piece of iron over a fire and I stopped to watch. He used a foot pedal to blow air over the coals and heat them up. When the iron was red hot, he started bending it with a hammer.

"What are you making?"

"Gate hinges."

I watch him make the hinge. To me, it's beautiful.

I watched that worker bending hinges for hours. By the end of the day, I was sure I could do it myself.

Next morning, when we arrived at the foundry, the SS man had another Heftling with him. Not a kid, but an older man.

"This man will show you how to work with iron. He will be your instructor."

I took one look at the guy – he was an ironworker like my grandmother was an ironworker. He could probably instruct us Talmud, but he wouldn't know which end of a hammer to hit with. One of the other kids recognized him as a rabbi from his old village. The kind-hearted SS officer probably chose him because he was incapable of heavy labour.

But the rabbi was a bright man, and even though he could give us no practical instruction he gave us a good theoretical grounding in ironwork. Iron is extremely malleable – you can bend it into almost any shape if you get it hot enough – and the faster you cool it, the better it holds that shape.

That was all the instruction I needed. While the others were still learning how to make a fire, I was an expert at making knives. To make a knife that would hold an edge, you had to cool it in ice-cold water.

"Get me some water before I make it hot," I would tell my helper.

After the knife cooled off, I sharpened it on a stone.

Making knives was hard work, but I loved it.

It lasted about a month.

Then the SS officer was replaced and we all went back to unloading bricks.

—

The heavy labour and lack of food were harder on my father than they were on me. He started getting dizzy spells. He never complained, but I could tell something was wrong. After work, I looked for him at the *Tzail Appel* so that I could line up beside him and we could walk back to camp together. These days he was walking more and more slowly. One hot day in the middle of summer, he could hardly walk at all. When we got back to the camp from the work site, he was ready to collapse.

"I have to go to the hospital. I can't stand up."

I watch him walk to the hospital building. He's very unsteady on his feet.

My father was admitted to the hospital, suffering from malnutrition. Everyone was suffering from malnutrition, but going without food is harder on some people than on others. My father was not a sickly person, he was a healthy man with a healthy appetite. The only time he'd ever been in the hospital was a number of years earlier when he had a stomach ulcer operation. As a young man, he couldn't eat tomatoes, but since the operation he could eat anything. Now he had nothing to eat and was back in the hospital.

One of the older Heftlings told me what that meant.

"If he doesn't get better in a few days, they'll ship him back to Birkenau."

"What happens there?"

"What do you think happens? If you can't work, you're no good to them."

He wasn't being inhuman – he was just preparing me for the blow. The Heftlings did not kid each other. If you asked a question, you got the answer. The truth was hard to deal with, but it was better than holding false hope. If you expect the worst, you might be able to deal with it.

The minute I got back from work, I'd go to the hospital to see my father, whose bed was by the window. I'd bring him a bowl of soup, a piece of cheese – once I even managed to bring him cigarettes. That night we'd been given a slice of liverwurst, or some other delicacy, and one Polish guy wanted to trade. He offered me two cigarettes and something else that I don't remember. Food was our currency – a piece of smelly cheese was worth so much; a piece of liverwurst was worth so much. Everything had a certain value.

My dad was so happy to have a smoke that he hugged me. It was his last smoke – the next day he was gone. I'll never forget it.

I'm standing outside the window, looking at his empty bed.

Then I see the truck by the hospital entrance. The motor is running and it's already loaded with Heftlings, some standing, others sitting. There's a gate across the back of the truck and I don't see my father.

Then I see his head through a space between the boards of the gate.

I start to cry.

He turns and looks at me.

I stand there, crying, with my father looking at me for what seems like an hour.

Finally the truck drives away.

I lie down on the ground and cry.

It's a hot day and the ground is sandy.

Nobody pays attention to me. They have their own troubles.

Eventually an older heftling comes up to me and tries to console me in Yiddish.

"You never know – sometimes, sometimes …"

Sometimes a miracle happens – that's what he means.

But I don't believe in miracles.

My father was forty-four years old when he died. We'd been in the camp for about four months. I don't know the exact date – it was late summer. I light a candle for him at the end of every August.

—

The day after my father died does not stand out in my memory. Nothing made it memorable. I now drank my tin of coffee alone and walked to and from work alone; otherwise, it was business as usual. My life had been hopeless before and it was still hopeless. Every day in the camp was the same as every other day. The only thing that changed was the weather.

Summer dragged into fall and fall dragged into winter. Now, in addition to our other burdens, we had to cope with the cold. Heftlings were no longer dying just of hunger and exhaustion but of hypothermia. With no fat to burn, you couldn't keep warm no matter how many layers of clothing you put on. The only fuel we had was low-grade coal. While we unloaded the flatcars, our foreman warmed himself by a small coal-burning stove. There was a coalfield on the other side of the yard, and when the bucket was empty he would send one of us to refill it. We all wanted to go because it meant a short break from unloading the cars.

One day, he chooses me.

"You, get some coal."

He doesn't have to tell me twice. I pick up the pail and head for the coalfield.

I can hardly bend over to pick the coal up from the ground so I sit down and begin tossing it into the pail. I make a game of it. Sometimes I hit the pail, sometimes I miss.

Then suddenly I see a German SS officer a long way off.

He is coming toward me, shaking his finger.

I jump up and start working faster.

The pail fills up.

I pick it up and start to leave.

But the SS officer yells at me.

"Vart (Wait)! Vart!"

So I wait.

He's a young punk with blond hair and rosy cheeks.

"I don't know where you come from, but in Germany we don't work like this. What you were doing isn't work."

He makes a fist and comes toward me.

I wake up and think I'm in my bunk.

But I'm on the ground.

I sit up and look around.

Where am I?

I see a pail lying on its side, with some coal spilled out.

I put the coal back into the pail, pick it up, and start walking.

Where am I going?

I can't remember.

I see railroad cars and remember my errand.

The foreman didn't look happy to see me.

"Where in the hell were you?"

"At the coalfield."

"All this time? What happened to your face?"

"I was hit by an officer."

"Why?"

I tell him.

"So why didn't you come back after he hit you?"

"I fell down."

"Were you unconscious?"

"I don't remember."

"Well, you've been gone for four hours!"

I expect him to hit me, but he just shakes his head.

"You probably deserved what you got. Now get back to work."

So I got back to work.

⸻

The days grew shorter, the snow began to fall, and we could hear the sound of bombs and machine gun fire in the distance. The Russians were coming! Groups of Heftlings would stand around and speculate on how close they were. Sometimes there would be a *dogfight*. We'd stand in the yard and watch the planes buzzing overhead like bees. A murmur of approval would buzz through the camp every time a German plane headed for the ground, trailing smoke. But our Nazi masters made it clear that even the arrival of the Russians wouldn't help us.

"Don't get your hopes up," they would shout at us, "because you're not going to survive!"

We hoped they were bluffing, but we didn't kid ourselves. A cornered rat is more dangerous than a confident "Superman." These Nazi bastards in their fancy uniforms were more frightened than their victims. Their smug superiority had given way to panic. The SS were perfectly capable of destroying us all to hide the evidence of their crimes. So we didn't let ourselves get too hopeful. Every time we heard machine gun fire, we would whisper among ourselves, but the word "liberation" was never mentioned.

—

Once the *Block Eldster* locked the door, it stayed locked until the whistle sounded next morning. So when someone woke me up in the middle of the night, I knew something was wrong. I sat up and saw a *Kapo* standing at the front of the block. "Wake up," he ordered. "We are going to march. Get dressed warm. Put on two pairs of pants!"

I put on all the clothes I had. From somewhere, I don't remember where, I got an extra jacket that wasn't like the others; it was all grey with just a small blue and white striped patch on the back. I put that one on top because I didn't look so much like a Heftling when I wore it. At least that's what I told myself. One look at me was enough to tell anyone what I was.

When I went outside, it was still dark. There is no *Tzail Appel*, just hundreds of people running around while a voice blares over the loudspeaker. "We are evacuating the camp. Everybody must go – no exceptions! Even the sick must try to march. The camp will be destroyed! There is no use trying to hide; we are blowing up the buildings!"

I wandered around, trying to get my bearings. Every Heftling in camp was outside, including some I seldom saw during the day. I saw a kid from my hometown whose skin was so black I barely recognized him in the dark. He'd been working in the coal mine. It was such a terrible job that the Heftlings doing it had special privileges – a little more to eat, a little better treatment.

"You should volunteer too," he had suggested when we first arrived. But I didn't want to be separated from my father. And I didn't think it was worth doing that kind of work for an extra crust of bread.

The loudspeaker continues to blare as I wander around.

"Everyone who is ready to march will get a loaf of bread...."

A whole loaf! I can't believe it. I figure it's just another one of their lies. But I see they have opened the gate to the magazine and a Kapo is standing there, handing out loaves of bread.

I take and loaf and put it under my coat.

As I go to line up, I see someone else from my hometown – a shoemaker about my father's age – standing in front of the hospital, not moving. I call out to him.

"Get a loaf of bread. We're going to march."

He doesn't move – just continues to stand there, as if he's about to fall on his face.

When he speaks, his voice is so weak I can hardly hear him above the racket.

"I can't go."

"You have to, they're going to blow up the hospital!"

"There's nothing I can do. I can't walk."

As we march out of the camp, he stays behind.

I am sure I will never see him again.

I was wrong. When I finally returned to Beregszasz several months later, the shoemaker was already there. The SS were so anxious to run away from the Soviet troops that they didn't bother destroying anything. When the Russian tanks rolled in, the soldiers found the camp exactly as we had left it. Being too sick to leave with the rest of us was the luckiest thing that ever happened to the shoemaker from Beregszasz. If he hadn't stayed behind to be "blown up," he would never have survived an ordeal that was worse than anything we had yet experienced.

DEATH MARCH

The mass evacuation of a legion of half-dead human beings from slave labour camps in occupied Poland to older concentration camps in Germany, in the middle of winter, is known as "the death march." It's a fitting name. We were given a choice: "March or die." My miserable childhood, the loss of my siblings, riding a cattle car to Auschwitz, helplessly watching my father drive away in the back of a truck – these are painful memories. The death march is something I still live with. It is a continuing nightmare:

As we march out of camp, it is so dark I can't make out individuals, just a moving mass of walking corpses, strung out along a country road. As the night wears on, the gaps in the line become bigger – and the guards farther apart.

My father is gone, my "friends" have disappeared, and I am walking by myself.

Suddenly someone grabs my arms from behind. There are two of them, one on each arm, and a third has his hand inside my coat. I try to fight but it's no use. They give me a couple of shots that make my head swim.

Then they disappear into the night with my bread.

Not every Heftling was an innocent victim; some were criminals. Others had a criminal mentality – they were law-abiding people who shared the Nazi philosophy that it is "natural" for the strong to devour the weak. I do not claim to be an altruistic person – once my father perished, I didn't worry about anyone but myself – but victimizing a fellow Heftling in order to survive never crossed my mind.

Yet I survived the death march while many of the victimizers perished.

How long did we march?

I have no idea.

All I know is that we marched day after day, night after night, through town after town, with no chance to rest and nothing to eat. Hitler's pets, the Waffen SS, knew what lay in store for them if the Soviets caught up with them, so they were running for their lives. The Soviet tanks were rolling in from the east, and American tanks were rolling in from the west. The SS had chosen the lesser of two evils. They knew the Americans would abide by the laws of the Geneva Convention. The United States hadn't been invaded, the soldiers' homes burned down, their wives and daughters raped, their parents and children slaughtered. Most American soldiers were under the illusion that they were fighting a "civilized" war.

Russian soldiers were under no such illusion. They would shoot any captured SS officers like vermin. So the rats were deserting a sinking ship. They drove us across the country, in the dead of winter, at an inhuman pace. People would fall and get up, fall and get up, fall and get up – until they could no longer get up. We would march around them. Then, a few seconds later, we would hear a short burst of machine gun fire, like a burp. The SS didn't want to take a chance on leaving any of their victims alive.

But even a dead body can speak, so a horse and wagon followed us to keep the road "clean." The Nazi murderers wanted to destroy all evidence of their crimes before the Allies arrived. If what went on in the death camps came to light, even the Americans might start shooting the SS like the mad dogs they were – which is why they evacuated our camp in the middle of the night.

When it started to get light, we stopped to rest by the side of the road, next to a farmer's field. Some of the Heftlings ate bread but since I had no bread, I just sat there looking out across the field. It was all ploughed up, and I wondered what the crop was.

The guy beside me, a Polish kid about my age, told me.

"Sugar beets."

We look at each other with the same thought.

"Maybe they missed some."

We look around, see that the guard isn't watching, and crawl out into the field on our stomachs.

I find a few dried-up beets lying on the ground, covered with mud.

I wipe one off and take a bite.

It's frozen solid.

Unlike many of the Heftlings, I still have good teeth, so I chew the beets until they get soft, swallow the juice, and spit out the pulp.

It doesn't stop the hunger pangs but it gives me a bit more energy.

After a few hours, fresh SS men with machine guns got us back to our feet. The guards changed every few hours and were always fresh. They marched us night and day. How I survived is a miracle. I couldn't stand on my feet. All I wanted to do was lie down on the ground, close my eyes, and never have to open them again. I lost all track of time. It was an endless nightmare of which I only remember isolated incidents.

I am marching beside a kid about my age. At least I think he's my age – with the Heftlings, it's hard to tell. This kid is probably half his former size.

Suddenly he says something that I'm thinking.

"I can't walk anymore."

Before I know it, he's running across a field.

I hear a guard behind me shout to him.

"Halt!"

He keeps running.

I hear gunfire.

The kid falls, face forward.

I see a red stain on his back.

He's out of his misery.

My misery continued. Hour after hour, day after day, step after step. I began to think that I would be better off if they shot me too. But they didn't shoot me – even when I couldn't march anymore.

At one point in the march, I passed out. I don't know how long I was unconscious, but when I came to I was still marching, but not under my own power – there were two Heftlings holding me up by the arms. I couldn't believe it. Why were these guys carrying me?

I didn't get a chance to find out.

As soon as they saw that I could walk on my own, they disappeared, fast.

To this day I don't know what happened. I can only assume that when I fell down a German guard, who had a fondness for children, didn't want to shoot me. So he made two of the older Heftlings pick me up and carry me. They certainly wouldn't have done it on their own. People were being shot like flies and nobody even turned to look. Why was I singled out for special treatment? It's something I have wondered about for half a century.

—

Yavoshno was not the only camp being evacuated. As we marched west toward the German border, we passed other camps that were also being cleared out. Wherever there was a factory, there was a slave labour camp nearby. One small camp called Bunai was near a paint factory. Blechemar, an older camp with concrete fences, razor wire, and high guard towers, was being used as a rest stop. As the SS marched us toward the gate, just as it was getting dark, another contingent of Heftlings was marched out.

In spite of my exhaustion, I can't sleep. There are warplanes dogfighting overhead. And Katyusha rockets keep blowing up buildings. So far, nothing has landed near us. The Russians seem to know which buildings are SS headquarters. But a rocket can go astray. Our liberators could easily kill us. Still, it's a comfort to know they are so close.

When I get up to relieve myself, I see people moving around, looking out the window, whispering.

I go to the window to see what's going on.

"Look," one of them says, pointing.

I look out the window. There is no one in the guard tower.

I look around the yard, which is flooded with light, and I see there isn't a German soldier anywhere.

It takes a minute to sink in.

Then everyone gets excited.

"We're free! We're free!"

People start running out the door.

I follow them.

As I get closer to the door, I hear the sound of a machine gun.

I duck out of the doorway, go back to the window, and look out.

Some Heftlings are lying on the ground, others are falling.

The rest come scrambling back into the block.

"The SS are at the gate. They're shooting anyone who tries to escape."

Maybe I should let them shoot me too. It would be easier than starving to death.

Just across the road from our block is a magazine. I can see it through the window. The door is open and people are walking out with tin plates of food.

Three of us decide to risk it.

We go out the door and start running.

A machine gun rattles.

The guy in front of me falls down.

I trip over him.

He's lying still, not moving.

I crawl around him on my stomach, using my elbows.

A machine gun rattles again.

I don't know if they are shooting at me or someone else.

I keep crawling and make it to the magazine.

I go inside and come out with a tin plate of sauerkraut – the only thing they have left.

I pick some up with my fingers and put it in my mouth.

I can't swallow it. It's too strong.

I spit it out.

The other Heftling who has also risked his life for this delicacy can't believe his eyes. "What are you doing?" he asks.

"I can't eat it," I say. "It will burn my stomach out."

"So give it to me."

I hand him the plate and he shovels it in.

Later that night, back in the block, he keeps me awake with his moaning.

"Oy vay! Oy vay!"

He cries for hours.

Then suddenly he stops.

In the morning, the SS get their flunkies to drive up the wagon and load him onto the pile. Another dead Jew – no big deal.

—

Next morning, when the Germans came back into camp to march us out, they weren't all SS officers; some were regular army, and there were even a few local policemen. They weren't as rough as the SS or as disciplined. But even the SS were losing their composure. Their orderly world was crashing in on them and they couldn't cope. There was gunfire in the distance, soldiers were shouting, Heftlings were milling about – it was chaos.

Some Heftlings had cut a hole in the wall with picks they'd found.

Others had hidden.

But when the order came to line up and march out, I did what I was told.

—

We marched for another five or six days, through town after town, until we reached Breslau, an East German city just over the Polish border. By this time, thousands of Heftlings from other camps had joined us, some from my hometown. For a few days, I marched beside Irving "Itzik" Izcovitch, the hustler who used to sell chocolate powder in *cheder*. He was about five years older than I was and thought he knew all the angles. When he saw that under my Heftling uniform I was wearing a jacket that didn't have blue and white stripes, his eyes lit up.

"Where did you get that?" he asks.

"They gave it to me," I say. "Why?"

"If you wear that jacket on top no one will know you're a Heftling. You can escape."

"You're crazy," I say. "It's got a patch on the back with stripes."

"So you'll take the patch off. If I had a jacket like that, I'd be gone in a minute."

"And you'd be shot in a second."

"So what do you think they're going to do when we get to Germany, make us a party?"

I'm afraid of getting shot, but he keeps bugging me. Mile after mile, he keeps it up.

"You're just a kid. Maybe someone will take pity on you and hide you until the Russians get here. They're just a couple of days away."

We stopped for a rest at a spot with a ditch alongside the road. The guards weren't SS officers with machine guns but old Wehrmacht soldiers who looked like they couldn't hit the side of a barn with their rifles.

I decide to take a chance.

When the guards aren't looking, I roll into the ditch and lie down as flat as I can.

And wait …

Usually, the rest periods were over almost before we sat down, but this one seemed to last forever. My face was pressed against the frozen ground, and my heart was pounding in my ears. Finally I heard the order to resume the march.

I hold my breath and keep my head down.

I hear people getting to their feet.

I decide to wait ten minutes for them to get out of sight.

I count off the seconds.

Eventually, all I can hear is the sound of my own breathing.

I lift my head just high enough to see over the edge of the ditch.

The marchers are a few hundred yards down the road.

As soon as the marchers were out of sight, I stood up and looked around. There was a farmhouse in the distance, and I went up to it and knocked on the door. A woman's voice answered in German.

"I'll be right there."

I wait, shivering, for her to open the door.

The well-dressed woman in her thirties who opened the door didn't look like a farmer's wife, more like the wife of an officer. When she saw who was standing in her doorway, her pale blue eyes turned to ice.

"What are you doing here?"

I don't answer, just walk past her into the house.

She closes the door behind me to keep out the cold air.

"Are you with that group that just went past?"

I nod.

Her eyes grow even harder.

"In this country criminals can't run free. I'll have to call the police."

She goes to a crank phone and starts cranking.

I move back toward the door.

"Just wait," she says, holding up a finger.

So I wait. Where can I go?

She cranks and cranks and finally gets someone on the line.

She talks to the person in German then hangs up.

I'm so weak I can hardly stand.

"Can you give me something to eat?"

"I have nothing to eat."

"Can I sit down?"

She doesn't answer.

I sit down on a kitchen chair.

She sits down on another chair.

We sat in silence for a long time. Then I heard a motorcycle pull up outside. The woman opened the door and let in a young policeman. When he saw me, he looked upset. "He's an escaped Heftling," the woman said, but the policeman didn't give her the pat on the back she expected.

"How long has he been here?"

"About an hour."

"Did you give him anything to eat?"

The woman shakes her head.

The policeman glares at her.

"Why not? He's a young kid! Can't you see he's starving?"

The woman turns red in face.

"Well, I guess I can make him something...."

She made me a couple of pieces of bread and butter. While I'm eating, the policeman tries to talk her into hiding me on the farm.

"The Russians will be here soon. Do you know what they do to German women? If you save this boy, you'll have something to tell them."

"How can I hide him? I'm not alone here; I have workers."

He saw that he was wasting his breath, so he apologized to me.

"I have to take you back."

We rode back on his motorcycle. On the way, he stopped by the side of the road to eat his lunch. He took a sandwich out of his saddlebag but couldn't eat it in front of me.

"Are you still hungry?"

What a question!

He tore his sandwich in half and shared it with me. He also shared his thoughts.

"This woman doesn't have a brain in her head. She's a real Nazi."

When we caught up with the group, they were resting.

One of the guards ran up to us, very excited.

"What happened?"

The policeman answers calmly.

"Nothing, he just straggled behind. You missed him."

The soldier kicks me in the behind.

The policeman intervenes.

"Let him alone. He didn't hurt anyone; he was just trying to save his life."

The guard walks away.

The policeman climbed on his motorcycle and went back the way he came. I stood there, looking around in disbelief. All the Heftlings were sitting on the ground eating boiled potatoes in the skins. A soldier noticed me standing around and came up to me.

"Why aren't you eating?"

I look at him and don't know what to say.

"Come with me."

I follow him to a huge pot.

He reaches inside and pulls out five potatoes.

It was unbelievable! I was already full and he was offering me five potatoes.

I put them inside my coat for later.

Forty years later I finally got the chance to tell Itzik Izcovitch what had happened to his plan. He was living in Los Angeles, selling used cars. He wasn't at home when I called, so I went out to the dealership. When I saw him, after all this time, I was so overcome with emotion that I couldn't talk.

Neither could he.

"Not now, I've got a customer."

The leopard hadn't changed his spots!

When Itzik finished hustling his customer – he didn't make the sale – I told him my story about the lady on the farm. He couldn't believe anyone would turn in a little kid. He told me that later he and another guy had also walked away from the march.

"Just like you, we went up to a farmhouse and knocked on the door."

"What happened?"

"They were glad to see us."

It's all fate – he and his friend had picked the right house and their nightmare had ended.

I had picked the wrong one so mine continued.

―

We marched into Breslau, two thousand scarecrows down the main street. The local people looked out their windows to watch the parade, but it didn't bother me – I was too weak and hungry to worry about such things. My potatoes had run out days ago.

We walked through the city to the railway station where a guard gave us some good news.

"The march is over. From here, you go by train."

"Where are we going?"

"Buchenwald."

—

The train to Buchenwald was not like the one that took us to Birkenau – it had open cars with wooden slats on the sides. As they loaded us aboard, I felt a sense of relief. It was snowing out, but at least we would be able to breathe in this car. And they didn't jam us in so tightly; there was room to sit down. The floor was covered in some kind of gritty substance, but I was so grateful for the chance to sit down that I didn't pay any attention to it.

After a few hours, the train starts to move.

And my backside starts to itch. I try to ignore it.

As we travel through the city, we go under a number of pedestrian overpasses.

People stop and look down at us – literally as well as figuratively.

"Heftlings."

After sitting on the wet floor for a few minutes, my backside is no longer itching, it's burning. People all around me are getting to their feet. Finally I can't stand it any longer and get to my feet too. But my backside continues to sting. And I'm not the only one. Everyone is jumping around. It's like we've been sitting on a wasps' nest. What the hell is that stuff on the floor? Then someone figures it out.

"These cars have been used to haul salt!"

The melting snow had wet the salt, which had eaten through our pants and burned our flesh. Sitting on the floor was like sitting in an acid bath.

So we all had to stand for the entire trip – four days with nothing to eat. People were dropping all around me. Some would get up; others stayed on the floor despite the salt.

On the second or third day – I'm not sure, I've lost count – a guy standing next to me falls down. I wait for a few minutes to see if he gets up.

He doesn't.

Is he dead or just unconscious?

I wait for awhile longer.

Then I sit down on his leg.

He doesn't move.

I breathe a sigh of relief.

I had a place to sit for the rest of the trip.

—

Buchenwald was a huge camp with hundreds of blocks – like a small city. As the soldiers unloaded us from the train and marched us through the gate, we passed a nicely painted building. Teenage kids were looking out the window, watching us. Not German kids, but Jewish kids.

It's like a dream.

These Jewish kids are wearing clean white shirts and have fat faces.

Then I recognize one of the faces – it belongs to my fourteen-year-old cousin, Sholi Blau. He looks as healthy as he had when he was raking straw on my Uncle Zindli's farm.

He looks at me without acknowledging me.

Maybe it is a dream – or a hallucination.

The soldiers marched us to a block at the back of the camp. It took about half an hour to get there, and it was a different world. Then the strange dream was replaced by a familiar nightmare. The Block Eldster, a Czechoslovakian Communist, was very sympathetic, but sympathy was all he had to offer us.

"Food I can give you when they bring it."

For the first three days, they didn't bring it. Every morning I'd wake up and someone else would be dead from malnutrition. The rest of us were skin and bones. It takes a long time to starve to death. As long as you have water, you can keep on going.

So I kept going.

The camp was so well guarded that they let us walk around. I wandered around all day, looking in garbage cans for food. Once I found a few potato skins. I chewed on them but couldn't swallow. In another can, I found a hunk of raw meat that looked like a dog's hind leg.

Before I have a chance to examine it, some Heftlings snatch it out of my hand.

They build a fire and cook it.

I eat some.

One day the Block Eldster offers me a bowl of soup that has turned sour.

"I can't eat this. Do you want it?"

I gobble it down. It's delicious!

As I wander around the camp, eating garbage and spoiled soup, I keep thinking about those fat faces in the window. I know it wasn't a hallucination because others saw them too. So I keep asking people about them.

"Who are those kids?"

Nobody knows the answer.

—

Thirty years later, I finally solved the mystery. I was in Florida on my first winter vacation, and I looked up my cousin Sholi, whom I hadn't seen since Buchenwald. I asked him why he hadn't acknowledged me when I arrived.

"I didn't notice you. They were bringing trainloads in from the camps every day – Jews, Hungarians, Russians. We used to stand at the window and watch them go by. And they all looked the same, like skeletons."

"How come you looked so nice? Healthy, well-dressed.…"

"Erno, our block was a showplace for the Red Cross. Every week we had visitors. They would ask us questions and we'd tell them the truth. We were well fed, given nice clothes to wear, books to read – we had a hell of a good life. We couldn't tell them what went on in the other parts of the camp because we weren't allowed to go there. And neither was the Red Cross. From the hundreds of blocks in Buchenwald, our ideal block was the only one that was shown to the inspectors.

"And they were prepared to accept that?"

"Erno, they didn't give a damn about the Jews. The Geneva Convention said they had to inspect, so they inspected what Hitler was prepared to show them."

—

By the spring of 1945, the destruction that Germany had inflicted on her European neighbours was being returned tenfold. Hitler's war of expansion was being waged in his own backyard. While the Nazi superman hid in his underground bunker, wave after wave of bombers pounded the shit out of the helpless people he claimed to love so fervently. Hitler could have stopped the carnage with the stroke of a pen; instead, he ordered a scorched earth policy – the destruction of anything that could be used to rebuild Germany after the war. He justified his twisted priorities in his will.

"If the war is lost, the people will also be lost. In any case only those who are inferior will be left after this struggle."

Now that the handwriting was on the wall. Adolph Hitler, the great warrior-philosopher, was concerned with the fate of only one German – himself. While he hid like a mole in his underground bunker, the bombs continued to fall on his "inferior" people.

⌐

The world was blowing up around us. Every day we saw airplanes fighting overhead and heard artillery shells exploding in the distance. One night the whole ground shook from falling bombs. The *Block Eldster* kept us informed.

"Those are the Americans. They're bombing the SS living quarters."

How could the Americans tell one building from another? How could they even see the camp from the air? We were in the middle of a forest. The Americans were on our doorstep, but nobody was rejoicing. You could die on the last day of a war as easily as on the first.

The *Block Eldster* was very sympathetic, but he didn't give us false hope.

"You people are Jews. You are in danger of being killed before the Americans get here."

Even though the war was in its final days, the mood in the block remained sombre.

⌐

One morning I wake up to an unusual sound.

It's machine gun fire. The Americans must be close because you never hear machine guns from far away, just the sound of big guns.

The guy in the next bunk hears it too.

"Do you know what this means?"

He jumps out of bed, falls on his face, and doesn't have the strength to get up. He lies on the floor, bleeding from the mouth, while other Heftlings go to the window and look out.

I get up and join them.

There's nothing to see.

We stand there looking for a while, then go back to our bunks.

People looked out the window all day, but they didn't see anything out of the ordinary. The day dragged by like any other.

The next morning I got up and looked out the window again.

Still nothing.

Later that afternoon, I'm looking out the window when I see something move in the bushes.

I keep looking.

I see an SS officer walking with his hands up, holding a machine gun in one hand.

There is a tank behind him.

"Come look!"

Everyone rushes to the window to see the show.

The top of the tank opens up.

A soldier with a black face pops out and points his pistol at the SS officer.

I think he's going to shoot the German bastard, but he just makes him hand up his machine gun.

The black soldier hands the machine gun to someone in the tank and gives an order.

The German turns around and starts walking in our direction, his hands over his head.

The tank follows right behind him.

I've never seen a tank like this – it has a big star on the front.

LIBERATION

The American army liberated Buchenwald without firing a shot. As soon as the Nazis saw that the camp was surrounded, they dropped their weapons and threw up their hands. Within a few hours of sunrise, all our SS guards had been rounded up and marched away. Nothing else happened for the rest of the day. We had been liberated, but we still went to sleep hungry.

The first thing I saw the next morning was a Jeep flying a Red Cross flag. We all went outside to meet it. Medics jumped out of the Jeep and told us what was going to happen. In a couple of hours, they were going to bring in soup for us. "That's all you're going to get until your digestive systems are working properly," the medics explained. At the time I was disappointed, but later I was grateful. In the camps that the Russians liberated, , starving Heftlings were allowed to gorge themselves on rich food, and many died in agony. One of them was a cousin of mine, whose kidneys had shut down. Then typhus broke out and hundreds more died.

At Buchenwald, after the liberation, the only people who died were the ones who were beyond saving.

Our liberators imposed discipline and hygiene. The Americans were beautiful. When they took over the camp, it was like a holiday. Everyone smiled and hugged the soldiers, some of whom were Jewish. They separated the children from the adults and, once we were able to tolerate rich food, brought us chocolate bars. In exchange for the chocolate, they collected souvenirs.

"Do you have any binoculars?"

The American soldiers all wanted German binoculars.

Buchenwald was just a few kilometres from Weimar, and the Americans took us there on bus tours. But they wouldn't let us off the buses. They knew better than to let us mingle with the local Germans. The Russians had given liberated Heftlings an open field, and they had gone out and robbed and raped. I wouldn't have behaved in any more of a civilized manner. If the Americans had let me run loose on the streets of Weimar, I would have killed the first German I saw.

After the American Red Cross had brought us back to life, they had to figure out what to do with us. It was a tremendous problem. What do you do with a vast multitude of people, from all over Europe, who have been stripped of all possessions and have no family? The first step was to register everyone and find out where he or she wanted to go. Since English was the only language many of the Red Cross workers spoke, the better educated Heftlings acted as interpreters for the rest of us.

Politically active leaders emerged from the general population and tried to influence our decisions. The Communists said the Soviet Union was the land of milk and honey; the Zionists said Palestine was the only land that would welcome a Jew. They were both wrong. The Soviet Union was a totalitarian dictatorship, and Palestine would soon be off-limits to the Jews, thanks to a British embargo. Most of the Heftlings who opted for Palestine spent another few years in displaced persons camps and never set foot on Holy Land soil.

The American Red Cross gave us children the option of going to the United States, but not many chose to go. What did we know? America was a foreign country where we would be like fish out of water. Someone from my area of Hungary organized a group of children who wanted to go home. I was one of them.

As a going-away present, the Red Cross made us special uniforms: grey tailor-made suits with a small insignia on the jacket that said *Buchenwald Survivor*. They were nice suits and we were happy to wear them. We weren't ashamed of the insignia. It wasn't a yellow star; it was a badge of honour. We *wanted* people to know who we were. The Nazis treated us like criminals; the Americans made us feel like holy martyrs. Our suffering touched our liberators deeply. Battle-hardened soldiers would look at us and their eyes would fill with tears. They couldn't do enough for us.

And we couldn't do enough for one another. Now that we had no other family, our group of young survivors became like a family. We were loaded onto the back of a truck with long benches and driven to Prague, Czechoslovakia, which was now part of the Soviet Union. There, we were housed in a children's hostel, where we waited for leaders to arrive and take us to our different homes.

We spent a few days in Prague, sightseeing. The city, which hadn't suffered too much damage in the war, was still beautiful, and I felt at home there. Some people stared at us, but not with hostility. Everyone treated us with sympathy and respect. In Czechoslovakia, "Holocaust survivor" were magic words that could open doors. When we travelled by bus, we didn't have to pay; all we had to do was show our insignia. "We've paid already!" it said.

Although I was going back to Hungary, I would have preferred to live under a Czechoslovakian regime. To me, Czechoslovakia was a more civilized and tolerant nation. Our *Block Eldster* at Buchenwald – the one who had given me the sour soup – was a Czech from Prague. He was forced to do certain things in the camp, but he never acted maliciously. Whatever he could do to ease our suffering, he did. After the liberation, many *block eldsters* were beaten to death by the Heftlings; we carried ours on our shoulders. He came to visit us in the children's home in Prague. He was a hot Communist and would soon become a big shot in the government.

Our group from Buchenwald weren't the only war orphans in town. I sometimes saw other groups of Holocaust survivors walking and riding around. Even without our new suits, we weren't hard to recognize. But one day I saw a bunch of kids who looked too blond and healthy to be survivors.

As they march by in their fancy clothes, my curiosity grows.

I decide to ask a passer-by who they are.

"Hitler Youth," he says.

I feel my stomach turn over.

And I'm not the only one. "We don't have decent shoes to wear," one of my group says, "and these Nazi bastards are marching around in their fancy boots."

"Let's follow them and find out where they live," another guy says.

So we do. They are being held under house arrest in some kind of school or communal dormitory. That night about half a dozen of us decide to pay them a visit.

The door isn't locked so we walk right in.

When those blond sons of bitches see us they turn even paler.

"Who are you?" one of them asks in German.

"Who do you think we are?" our leader answers in German.

"Liberated?"

"That's right."

"What can we do for you?" the German kid asks politely.

"Take your boots off," our leader says.

The German kid sits down and takes them off. The rest of his buddies don't open their mouths; they just stand there and watch as a scrawny Jew boy steals their well-made German boots. Now that the shoe was on the other foot, if you'll excuse the pun, the Nazi super youth are frightened to death of us "inferior" types.

"We need shoes and pants," we tell them.

They open their suitcases.

Some of them don't move fast enough for one of the more belligerent guys in our group. He loses his temper. "Move faster, you murderers!" he yells, and slaps one of them.

They move faster.

It takes about half an hour to find something that fits. We're in the middle of going through their suitcases when the front door opens. "What's going on in here?" a man's voice says.

I look up and see two big bruisers. One is wearing a police uniform, the other is in civilian clothes.

"These Jews are trying to rob us," one of the German kids says.

The policeman looks at us. "Oh, these are Jews," he says, nodding.

"We're survivors," I say.

"Is that so?" he says, and smacks me in the face with his fist.

I spit out a tooth.

Ten minutes later we were thrown out the door, covered in bumps and bruises. I was bleeding from the mouth. As we staggered onto the sidewalk, a nicely dressed Czech couple stopped to talk to us. The woman was horrified by my appearance.

"Who did this to you?"

I answer in her native language, which is also mine.

"Your police." I tell her the story.

She can't believe it.

"Just because somebody accuses you of a crime doesn't give these men the right to beat you. We aren't under the Nazis now; even the police have to obey the law. You should file a complaint with their superiors."

She tells us how to get to the police station.

—

The police sergeant listened to our story with half an ear. He didn't even bother to write anything down, just interrogated us.

"Did you get their numbers?"

"No."

"Why were they there?"

"Someone must have called them."

"Who?"

"It must have been one of the German kids."

"What were *you* doing there?"

We told him the truth.

He thought it was a big joke. So what were we complaining about? When you put your nose where it doesn't belong, you shouldn't cry if it gets bloody.

But these were *policemen*! Weren't they going to be disciplined?

How could they be disciplined when we didn't have their numbers?

So the police weren't even going to investigate?

There was nothing to investigate – we got what we deserved.

—

I walked out of the police station with a broken heart. The sergeant's attitude hurt me more than the physical beating had. My father had loved this country, and the years he served in the Czechoslovakian army were the happiest of his life. Now the children of a former "enemy" could expect better treatment than his own son. I remembered what those Nazi bastards had said after their police "friends" had beaten us bloody. As we went out the door, one of them gave us a parting shot.

"Let this be a lesson to you. Nobody likes Jews."

These words have stayed with me.

HOME

The train ride from Prague to Beregszasz was an emotional experience. People were waiting at every station, anxious to see who would get off the train. People were hugging, kissing, crying – there were joyous reunions and crushing disappointments. The closer we came to the Hungarian border, the more anxious I became. Would there be anyone waiting for me?

Finally we pull into Beregszasz. I look out the window and see Herman and Layos Mihaly, two cousins on my mother's side, waiting in the station.

They were hoping to see a closer relative get off the train, but I am better than nothing.

—

Herman and Layos took me to another cousin's home, where they were living with what was left of my mother's family. All my uncles and aunts were dead, but some of their children had survived. I went with them only because I didn't have any other place to sleep.

My cousins treated me well, but I was uncomfortable living with them. They were all older than I was and tried to control my life. I was only fifteen years old but, after what I'd gone through, I was no longer prepared to be treated like a child, so I ignored them and did whatever I wanted. "I'm going to harness the horses and go for a drive in the wagon," I would say.

"No," they would say, "you can't."

I would do it anyway and they would chase after me, yelling.

"Come back! Come back!"

My cousins expected me to settle back down to a "normal life" just as if I had been away at summer camp. There was a sixteen-year-old girl who expressed an interest in me and they encouraged me to take advantage of the situation.

"Why don't you go out with her?"

So I would sit and talk to her. But while she was living on the moon, looking for boyfriends, I was still suffering from hunger pains. I wasn't interested in girls. Malnutrition had retarded my sexual desire as well as my physical development. When I bumped into old school friends on the street, they all looked younger rather than older. I must have looked the same to them. Instead of growing up and filling out, we had shrivelled up.

My physical immaturity was matched by my lack of emotional development. My cousins expected me to act like a young adult and make plans for the future, but I wanted to live out the boyhood I'd never had. My lack of responsibility drove them crazy. One incident almost caused my cousin Herman to hit me.

Shortly after I arrived, we got word that Romania was paying compensation to Holocaust survivors. King Michael of Romania was one of the few European leaders who had stood up to Hitler. While Hungary was shipping its Jews out of the country, Romanian Jews were standing on the railway platforms, handing up food. And now that the camps had been liberated, King Michael was offering to pay the survivors a certain sum of money – I don't remember how much – to get them back on their feet. All we had to do was travel 150 kilometres to a town in Romania to collect the money.

My cousins didn't want to give me my ticket, but since the train wasn't leaving until the afternoon they had no choice. We made arrangements to meet at the station. "Don't miss the train," they said, when I left the house in the morning. "Be there at least an hour before it leaves."

"Yeah, yeah," I said, and put the ticket in my pocket.

I don't remember what I did that day or where I went; I just remember one of my friends reminding me about the ticket in my pocket.

"Aren't you supposed to catch a train?"

By that time, the train was long gone.

I didn't care. Gone was gone. There would be another train.

A short time later, the border between Hungary and Romania was closed. My cousins had bought a ticket on one of the last trains.

Herman and Layos were ready to kill me.

"You've pissed away a once-in-a-lifetime opportunity!"

They might as well have talked to a wall. Money meant nothing to me. I was one of the lucky ones, and I was happy just to be alive and free. While the Jews of Eastern Europe were languishing in displaced persons camps, the Hungarian survivors had come home to pick up their lives where they had left off. We were the last to be shipped to the camps and the first to be repatriated. As soon as the Soviet army marched in, the Nazi collaborators had been tossed out on their ears. Confiscated homes and businesses had been restored to their former owners, and Jews were not only allowed to work but were given government jobs.

My cousins expected me to be a part of the new and thriving Jewish community in Beregszasz, but I had no such ambition. While my adult cousins were anxious to rebuild their lives, I had no life to rebuild. I was a backward fifteen-year-old with no mother, no father, no siblings, no education, no social skills, and no prospects. Everything had changed and nothing had changed. I was still living from day to day off the charity of my mother's relatives – people who could not understand my "irresponsible" attitude or tolerate my behaviour.

The only adult who had any patience for me was one of my father's former employees. Gaby – I don't recall his last name – had taken over my father's business. He offered to take me too.

"You'll come and live with us, work with me in the bakery, and someday you'll be the boss."

I was fond of Gaby, but baking bagels for the rest of my life didn't appeal to me. So I just moved into his home and bummed around with his wife's younger brother – another shiftless teenager. While my fellow survivors, who had no homes to go to, were living in displaced persons camps, I was living like a displaced person in my hometown.

Meanwhile a new Soviet society was being built around me. Army trucks drove up and down the streets, and any young man who didn't seem otherwise engaged was liable to be recruited into the rebuilding. One day a soldier jumped down from a truck and accosted me.

"Come with me; I have work for you."

"Thanks, but I'm not interested."

"I didn't ask if you were interested. There's work to be done."

He starts to get rough.

"It's okay, leave him alone."

I look around and see a Soviet officer emerge from the truck. He has a bunch of ribbons on his chest and looks familiar. He smiles at me.

"What's the matter, Erno? Don't you recognize me?"

It's my cousin Leibu Weiszberger!

Leibu was the son of my father's half-brother Ignac, who had the wood-turning shop across from the Hebrew school. I didn't tell Leibu about the joke the Hungarian soldier had made when his father was loaded into the cattle car. I just listened while he told me what had happened to his family.

"My father perished. But I ran away. I crossed the border and joined the Soviet army. Well, I didn't exactly volunteer. I was young so they took me."

He had fought on the Eastern front, become a highly decorated officer, and was now being sent to Czechoslovakia to study mechanical engineering. He had a bright future in the new Soviet society. In addition to a profession, he would no doubt acquire a wife and family. I was happy for him. When I was in the camps, that kind of "normal" life seemed like a dream.

But now that I was home, I had no desire to settle down. I was restless. Maybe I took after my father, who had been a bit of a drifter at my age. Even as an established family man, he was always looking for greener pastures. When Bereghovo became Beregszasz, I'd overhear him complaining to his cronies.

How can a man live in a country where the government changes every Monday and Thursday? And where every time there's a change in government, there's a change in policy? Where an established business can be snatched from you at any moment and put into the hands of a Gentile?

In Weisz Solomon's opinion, there was only one land where a Jew could feel at home. And that's where his son decided to go.…

"Nobody likes Jews"

As soon as the shooting war ended, the Cold War broke out. An Iron Curtain fell between Eastern Europe and the rest of the continent, which was cut up like a pie. There was a Soviet Zone, a British Zone, an American Zone – whoever got there first claimed their slice. Getting from Hungary to Palestine meant sneaking across borders, from zone to zone, like a thief in the night, until you reached Italy. Then you had to bribe the owner of a leaky boat to run the British blockade.

Those were the facts of life my friends and I had to face, according to the head of the Jewish Committee we had gone to see. "Palestine is a British Protectorate," he told the three of us, "and the British are protecting it from the Jews."

"What about the Balfour Declaration?" Duni asked.

The Jacobovitch family were hot Zionists, so Duni knew all about Lord Balfour and how the British foreign secretary had written a letter in 1917 expressing his government's approval of Zionism with "the establishment in Palestine of a national home for the

Jewish people." The purpose of this letter was to win the support of German Jews and neutral countries, such as the United States, for the British in the First World War.

But the British had a short memory. With the establishment of a Zionist state under British protection, the British gained possession of a strategic point on the land and sea routes to India, not to mention a terminus on the Mediterranean Sea for pipelines from the oil-bearing regions of the Middle East – which were controlled by the Arabs. During the Second World War, the British had trained an all-Jewish Palestinian Brigade to defend this strategic area, while the Arab nations had collaborated with the Nazis. But now *that* war was over too.

"Our British friends have no more use for us," we were told. "They have new friends."

The British were not going to alienate the Arabs just to please a bunch of sick and homeless European Jews. The Arabs were swimming in oil; Holocaust survivors didn't have a pot to piss in. Consequently, when the gates of the death camps burst open, the doors of the Jewish homeland slammed shut.

"*Aliyah* will take months or maybe even years," my friends and I were warned. *Aliyah*, a Hebrew word meaning "to go up," was used to describe emigration to *Eretz Yisroel* (the Land of Israel). "It's a young country and it needs young men, but you'll have to learn to speak Hebrew and build yourselves up physically. That's not something you can do on your own; you'll have to join a *kibbutz*."

My friends and I didn't have to think about it; we are all in agreement.

"Okay, so we'll join a kibbutz."

—

As the train pulls away, I look out the window and say goodbye to the city of my birth. I will never see these familiar buildings and landmarks again. The city hall where I pulled up weeds on my hands and knees; the office where I picked up a yellow armband; the schoolyard where I played soccer in bare feet, with a rolled up sock, while my classmates ate their lunches; the police station where I sat with my stepmother waiting to be deported to a country I had never seen – I have few fond memories to take with me and no family ties to bring me back. My cousins tried to talk me out of my hasty decision, but my mind was made up. I am looking forward to starting a new life with people who will welcome me with open arms, rather than shun me as an "outsider."

In Transit

Our first stop was Budapest, where we hooked up with a number of other survivors who would travel to Italy with us and the kibbutz *madrichim* (leaders). Seventy-five or eighty of us were making the journey. At the Austrian border, the *madrichim* had to find someone to smuggle us into the country, so we had some time to kill. I knew that a rich uncle on my mother's side whom I had never met lived in Budapest. This was a chance to meet him and his wife, but I didn't want to go alone so I took a friend.

I had no trouble finding his house – my cousins had given me the address – but getting through the door wasn't as easy. "Well, I guess you better come in," my uncle said after I had introduced myself. There were parcels and luggage all over the place. "We just got back," my uncle explained.

He and my aunt had been in an internment camp. Jews who had enough money to bribe the Hungarian officials weren't sent to Auschwitz but to an internment camp in Czechoslovakia. That's where my aunt and uncle had spent the last months of the war. And now they were unpacking their possessions.

My uncle took us into the kitchen and we sat down. There was food on the table, but he didn't offer us any. My aunt stuck her head through the kitchen door, saw us sitting around the table, and went back to her unpacking without saying a word.

After asking a few routine questions about what I was doing in town, my uncle stood up. "Well, I guess you have things to do," he said, going back to his unpacking. "Thanks for coming to see us."

"These people are your *relatives*?" my friend said, after the door had closed behind us. "The table is loaded with food and he doesn't even offer us a cookie?"

"They're all like that on my mother's side of the family," I said. "The ones on my father's side are nicer."

—

The Wandors had also just returned from the internment camp and were busy unpacking, but when they saw me at the door, they dropped everything. My aunt gave me a big hug, and my uncle invited us into the living room.

"Sit down. I'll make coffee."

My friend couldn't understand why these "Christian" relatives of mine had been in a camp. "I thought you said they weren't Jewish," he whispered to me.

My uncle, who was just returning with a tray of pastries, overheard him.

"As long as you have a drop of Jewish blood, to them you're a Jew," he said. "The only difference is that we wore white armbands instead of yellow."

"What about Mrs. Wandor?" my friend wondered out loud.

"I had to wear one too," she said, "because I married a Jew."

"I guess you're sorry you didn't listen to your father," my uncle said.

My aunt smiled. "It's no use crying over spilled milk."

"No, we were the lucky ones," my uncle said, looking at me. "If I didn't have the money to bribe the right people, Erno, I would have ended up in the same place as you and your father, may he rest in peace."

—

Later that night, one of the madrichim shook us from our sleep.

"Get up and get your stuff."

We travelled all night on foot, hiking through the forest, climbing up one mountain, sliding down another, and ended up in little town called Judenberg, not far from the city of Gratz, Austria. We have just arrived when our fair-weather "friends" round us up and march us off to an internment camp.

Welcome to the British Zone!

The head of the camp, a British major, was not happy to see us. Neither was the tough-talking sergeant he put in charge of our group – from him I learned my first English words: fucking Jews. We were taken to a large brick building that was once a residential school and assigned bunks. Then we were assembled in the courtyard where the major laid down the law.

He spoke to us through a translator – a black civilian who spoke perfect German – and made no attempt to hide his feelings. He talked to us as if we were scum. He didn't care who we were or what had happened to us in the past –while we were under his protection, we would follow the rules of the British military. Our barracks would be kept clean and orderly. There would be no fighting, arguing, or loud noise. We would be allowed to leave the camp during the day, but there was an eleven o'clock curfew.

The major's bark turned out to be worse than his bite. We violated curfew and nothing happened. Our British guardians couldn't be bothered to discipline a bunch of unruly "foreigners." The less they had to do with us the better. We didn't need the British anyway since we had our own disciplinarians. The madrichim kept us in line without resorting to threats. They reasoned with us. No one else would look out for us, they said, so we had to look out for one another. The good of the group had to be placed above our own selfish interests. That was the principle upon which *Shomer* was founded.

Collectivity was the underlying philosophy of all kibbutzim, but *Shomer Hatz'air*, the one I had joined, was the most extreme. We practiced a form of Marxism not even seen in the Soviet Union. There was no such thing as private property or personal possessions; everything belonged to the kibbutz. Money, food, clothing – everything went into the *Kupah* (pool) to be distributed as the need arose. No one would be cheated or dealt with unfairly. We had to trust one another.

My friend Duni was the ideal kibbutznik. The rules were no big change for him – he had grown up with loving parents and siblings who all looked out for one another. For me, trusting other people to look after my welfare was next to impossible. The only thing I had learned from my family life was how to look out for myself – especially when it came to my stomach.

Living conditions at the camp were tolerable, but food was scarce. I was always walking around Judenberg with a half-empty stomach, looking for something to eat. One day I was walking past a building when I saw something through the window that made me stop in my tracks.

"Did you see that?" I asked the guy walking with me.

"See what?" he said.

I pointed to the window. "There are Red Cross packages in there."

His face lit up and his mouth started to water. A package with a Red Cross on it meant only one thing – food.

We waited until the coast was clear then went inside the building and each took a package. We hid them under our beds and waited until everyone was asleep that night before we opened them and stuffed ourselves. There were cans of bacon, chocolates, all sorts of delicacies. We were having such a good time that we woke someone up.

"What's happening?" he says, sitting up in bed.

He looks around and sees what's happening.

"No, this isn't right! In Shomer you have to share."

That was the end of our midnight feast. The madrichim confiscated our "loot." My friend accepted the decision without an argument, but I was very put out. Why should we have to share our food with those who hadn't taken any risk?

"This is not your food. Even under the capitalist system you are not allowed to profit from a crime."

The madrichim did not appreciate my point of view. To me, stealing food wasn't a crime; it was a means of survival. I soon had another opportunity that was too good to pass up.

There was an orchard near the school that my friends and I couldn't ignore. We passed it every day on our way into town, and every day I would examine the crop to see if it was ready to pick. Now the apples were just turning red. One night when there was no moon, about six of us decided to raid the orchard.

It was pitch dark and no one was around, so we climbed over the fence.

I hit the ground and listen.

It's late summer and crickets are chirping.

I tied a shoelace around the bottoms of my pant legs, then climbed up a tree and started picking, dropping the apples down the front of my pants. My pants were almost full when suddenly I heard a commotion.

Dogs are barking, lights are shining.

"Stop! Police!"

I untied my pant legs to let the apples fall out and jumped down from the tree.

I hit the ground and start running.

A hand grabs my collar.

I break loose, hit the fence, jump over, and run like hell.

Three of us got away, but three of my friends were caught. The next morning I went to the police station to see them.

"No visitors," the desk sergeant told me. "Get out of here before I lock you up too!"

I go outside and see a basement window with bars on it.

I look through the window and see one of my friends sitting in a cell.

I call to him.

He comes to the window.

"Are you okay?"

He shrugs.

"They're feeding us."

Suddenly someone grabs my collar.

"What the hell do you think you're doing?"

I look up into a hostile face.

"Talking to my friend."

"He's your friend, eh?"

The Austrian cop marches me back into the police station.

"Sergeant, I caught another one of those orchard thieves!"

The sergeant looks up from his paperwork.

"How do you know he's one of them?"

"He's a friend of one of the guys you have in custody."

The sergeant looks at me.

"Weren't you just here a minute ago?"

I nod.

He gives me a hard look, as if he's trying to scare me.

"Were you one of the guys who raided the orchard?"

I shake my head.

"No."

He goes back to his paperwork.

"Let him go."

The police kept my friends in jail for nine days without bothering to bring them before a judge. Our British protectors didn't lift a finger to get them out. The major thought these fifteen-year-old kids had got what they deserved – nine days in an adult jail for stealing apples. When my fellow criminals were finally released, they looked as if they had each lost ten pounds. They walked into the barracks and we looked at each other. Nobody said anything, but we all had the same thought: *Let's get the hell out of this country!*

The madrichim were planning to cross into Italy, but because the British were keeping an eye on us they had to plan in secret. Maybe some of the older guys in the kibbutz were aware of what was going on, but I had no idea until one night we were told to get our backpacks ready.

"We're leaving in one hour."

The madrichim had paid a local Austrian to drive us across the border. We snuck out of the building in groups of five. It was a moonless night. After walking about a kilometre down the road, we came to a meeting place where a truck was waiting for us. It was the biggest vehicle I'd ever seen, with an enormous box and a huge tank on the front.

"What kind of truck is this?" I asked as I climbed into the back.

"A steam truck," a madrich said.

"Yeah, sure."

I thought he was kidding. He wasn't. During the war, Germany had manufactured thousands of steam trucks. They weren't as versatile as gasoline-powered vehicles, but they could generate enormous power and were ideal for transporting troops. The Nazis had a chronic shortage of gasoline – there are no oil fields in Germany – but an abundance of coal and an over-abundance of slave labourers to mine it. The coal powering this vehicle might have come from the camp that I had left.

The Austrian truck driver was very nervous. "Hurry up, hurry up," he kept saying, in German, as we climbed onto the back, "or I'll end up in jail. I'm taking a hell of a risk for you people."

"For the amount we're paying him," one of the madrichim said under his breath, "he can afford to take a few risks."

After we had all climbed aboard, we drove for a few hours to the outskirts of Gratz. Then the truck pulled over to the side of the road a few hundred yards from a railway station. The driver got out and came around to the back of the truck. "I have to fill up the boiler," he said. "We won't be stopping again for a long time, so you'd better do your business now."

He lowered the gate.

We all got off the truck to stretch and relieve ourselves.

Then the driver raised the gate and got back into the truck.

He didn't refuel; he drove away.

I was ready to kill him.

The madrichim had paid him a fortune to drive us to the Italian border, but they accepted this setback as the price of doing business.

"When you deal with lowlifes, you can't expect them to behave honourably."

So that the trip wasn't a total loss, we decided to get a few hours sleep.

—

It's the middle of the night and the railway station is deserted. Everyone is snoring. Some people are sleeping on the bare floor, using their backpack as a pillow, but I have a sleeping bag that I'm sharing with a friend. It's gotten quite cold, but that isn't what's woken me up. Someone is climbing into my sleeping bag.

It's Chana!

I can't believe it.

"She's just trying to get warm," I think as this beautiful eighteen-year-old girl squeezes between my friend and me.

But I'm not so sure. The girls of Shomer don't play games. They wear the same clothes as the boys, do the same work, and yield to the same impulses. Chana has discarded "middle class" conventions. It is not impossible that this older girl is attracted to me. I have grown and matured in the past few months. I am no longer a skinny kid but a handsome young man. Perhaps, if I do what comes naturally, I will lose my virginity.

—

I did not lose my virginity. What came naturally to others was unthinkable to me. Inside the handsome young man was a backward child who still occasionally wet the bed. I pretended I was asleep until the sun rose – and then got up to relieve myself.

Chana never mentioned this incident so her intentions remained a mystery, but when I got to know her better, I discovered that she was not only a beautiful young woman but a very fine person as well. She later became one of my teachers.

The next morning we rode to the border on the train. Nobody bothered us. We got off at a little mountain town where our leaders found someone who was willing to guide us across the Alps into Italy. When you had American dollars, you could always find people to help. But you couldn't always trust them.

This time our guide proved to be trustworthy. But the journey was tough all the same. We had to climb the mountains in the middle of the night and we couldn't see a damn thing. We just had to follow the person in front of us as we pushed through the trees. The guy in front of me kept letting go of the branches so that they slapped me in the face. He thought it was a big joke. We almost got into a fight, but one of the *madrichim* broke it up. They kept yelling encouragement.

"Keep going, keep going…."

Some of the girls didn't have the stamina, so we kept stopping to rest. A journey of a few miles took us the whole night.

—

As soon as we cross the Italian border, our guide disappears. We walk into a small border town just as the sun is rising and see a policeman on the street. On his head is a fancy hat with feathers that he's wearing sideways, like Napoleon.

"Wait here."

One of the madrichim approaches the policeman and talks to him.

Then I see the madrich hand him some money.

The policeman points.

The madrich comes back to the group.

"There's a place we can stay overnight."

I couldn't believe that a policeman would be so helpful. In the following months, I learned that Italians are not Austrians. Italy was to be my home for two years, and it will always hold a special place in my heart. In Italy, I learned to speak Italian as well as Hebrew and was treated like a worthwhile human being for the first time in my life. I had crossed the Alps, from darkness into light.

Kibbutznik

The difference between the British Zone and the American Zone was like night and day. There is a saying – when you do someone a favour, they never forgive you. I remain grateful for what the Americans did after the war. Today it is fashionable to criticize the United States for everything from its foreign policy to the treatment of its visible minorities. According to certain individuals and nations, "the land of the free" is a cynical exploiter of the weak. Someone is always ready to find fault with every move the world's last remaining superpower makes, and those who yell the loudest are often those who owe the country the most. The United States is not only the richest nation on Earth but also the most generous. Without an infusion of American dollars, war-torn Europe would have remained a wasteland for decades, and I would have remained a homeless wanderer.

—

We arrive at a transit camp in Milan, where refugees from all over Europe are being sent to different places

Jack, age 16

in Italy. Our group registers with the American Jewish Congress. There are maybe two dozen girls and women, half a dozen kids my age, and forty or fifty young men. After she takes our names, the Congress representative tells us we will be sent to a kibbutz in Grotto Ferrata.

"Where?"

"Grotto Ferrata. It's just outside of Rome."

We take the overnight train to Rome and buses and trucks the rest of the way. People from the kibbutz are waiting for us at Grotto Ferrata. We have to walk up a hill to get to our "barracks." I'm expecting some kind of residential school or other rundown institution, but instead I see a gorgeous villa.

"What is this place?" I ask.

"Villa Cicerona," a kibbutznik tells me.

The name means as much to me as Grotto Ferrata – which is nothing.

In the years leading up to the Second World War, Mussolini and Hitler tried to outdo each other in the propaganda war. Hitler had his pet movie director, Leni Riefenstahl, who created epic films in which the German Fuehrer and his Nazi cronies were portrayed as gods in human form. "Il Duce" built a 240-hectare movie studio in Rome, just east of the Appian Way, to grind out Italian potboilers glorifying himself and *his* degenerate regime. The studio, Cinecitta, was a stone's throw from Grotto Ferrata.

In the 1950s and 1960s Cinecitta would become known as "Hollywood on the Tiber" because of productions like *Cleopatra*, *Ben-Hur,* and *La Dolce Vita*. A few years after my departure from Italy, this famous studio would be home to Sophia Loren, Federico Fellini, and the brightest stars of Italian cinema. During the making of their movies, these actors and directors would stay at a nearby luxury resort called Villa Cicerona.

In the meantime, it was the temporary home of a bunch of Holocaust survivors.

Along with three other boys, I shared a third-floor suite that had a window overlooking a large swimming pool. There was no water in the pool; the girls used it to take showers. Water pipes had been run along the edge of the pool and the girls would stand under the pipes in the deep end, surrounded by a canvas screen and unaware that we could see them perfectly from the third floor. Our room became very popular with the rest of the boys. The windows had wooden shutters and we would watch the girls through the cracks. They tickled each other and grabbed at each other's breasts, and we would go into hysterics. It was quite a show.

But during the third shower, the girls heard us laughing.

The next day, the show was over – the *chayalim* (soldiers) extended the canvas screen to block our view.

A few of the madrichim at Grotto Ferrata were Holocaust survivors, but many were former members of the Palestine Brigade. Now that the war was over, the British had no more use for the all-Jewish brigade they had formed to protect their interests in the Middle East, so the chayalim had run home to see their families, from whom they'd been separated for years, then came straight to Italy to organize us. They were still wearing their British uniforms, minus the insignia.

Most of the chayalim were *Sabras* (native Palestinians) who, in addition to Hebrew, had some specialized knowledge or skill to pass on. They were extremely dedicated, intelligent, and accomplished individuals. (I remember one tall ex-colonel who had been a university professor.)

The idea was to prepare us for life on a kibbutz, so in addition to regular academic subjects, we had to learn a trade. We could choose from carpentry, metal work, and auto mechanics, but we were encouraged to take up agriculture. So that's what I chose. In addition to the chayalim, there were tradesmen working among us. A shoemaker who came from my hometown made shoes for everyone. (It took me eight months to get a new pair.)

The kibbutz was in a state of constant readiness as we waited to leave for Palestine. Since 1946, when the British had imposed a blockade, the only way to get into *Eretrz Yisroel* (the Land of Israel) was by way of *Aliyat Bet*, which was the Hebrew code name for illegal immigration. Aliyat Bet was the chayalim's job. They would smuggle groups of two or three hundred illegal immigrants across hostile borders into port cities in Italy or Greece, load them onto a fishing boat, and run the gauntlet of warships patrolling the waters off the Holy Land. It was a hazardous operation that had to be carried out with military precision, under cover of darkness.

If a boat was spotted, it had to turn back or its human cargo would end up in an internment camp in Cyprus. There was no way a fishing boat could outrun a British destroyer. The larger the boat; the less chance it had of running the blockade. The *Exodus*, a converted liner jammed with thousands of homeless Jews, was a sitting duck. It refused to turn back, so the British sunk it.

In spite of the dangers, there were always volunteers for aliyat bet. Duni's older brother, Moshe Jacobovitch, volunteered, and a few years later, Duni followed in his footsteps; they would both fight in the War of Liberation.

Moshe was a tough guy, but I couldn't see Duni as a soldier. He was so sensitive that he would faint at the sight of blood. But he wasn't shy – he loved to play the piano or get up and sing for people. He was very gregarious. He liked everyone and everyone liked him. Kibbutz life suited him perfectly.

It didn't suit me at all. I didn't trust anyone.

And after we were sent from Grotto Ferrata to Silvano, no one trusted me.

⁓

Our teachers' job was to re-educate as well as educate us. The Holocaust had been a wake-up call, and now the Jewish homeland needed a new type of Jew, one who was a soldier and a scholar. "Never again" would Jews go like lambs to the slaughter. If we were to survive as a people, we had to discard our ghetto mentality along with our ghetto language. The older generation had been wiped out, and now we had to rebuild a stronger and hardier generation.

It was difficult to accomplish this in a luxury villa on the outskirts of Rome.

Our Palestinian leaders thought it would be healthier for us children to be moved to a rural area. There was a *kinderhaim* (children's home) in Silvano, a little town in Northern Italy, near Milan. The madrichim held a *hasayfa* (meeting) to discuss it with us. How would we feel about going to the kinderhaim?

No one had any serious objections.

—

Within a few weeks, I was living near the Swiss border in a former private school that had been occupied by the Gestapo. Now it was a school for about three hundred young Holocaust survivors. First the teachers determined our grade level, then they designed our curriculum accordingly. I took classes in geography, mathematics, and other subjects, but we spent at least half our classroom time reading and writing *Ivrit* (Hebrew). The madrichim didn't teach from prayer books, as our cheder teachers had; they taught the "living" language that was spoken by the *chalutzim* (pioneers) in the Holy Land. Yiddish, the bastard child of the ghetto, was replaced by the ancient biblical tongue as the common language of three hundred young survivors from a dozen different European countries.

I had no trouble learning to speak *Ivrit*; otherwise, I didn't fit in too well. I felt like a fish out of water in the midst of all these strangers. I had no one to talk to and no time to myself. We got up at six in the morning and kept going from one communal activity to another until it was time to go back to bed. Everything was done in a group. You couldn't wipe your behind without a discussion and a vote. What type of toilet paper should I use? how many sheets? I couldn't get used to communal living. I found it impossible to sit through these endless discussions or quietly in class. The teachers from Palestine were very patient with me, but the survivors were from the "old school."

Every day began and ended with the raising and lowering of the blue and white *Mogen Dovid* (Star of David). As the flag was raised and lowered, the entire kibbutz would stand at attention and sing the Zionist anthem "Hatikvah" (Hope).

One morning, as the flag was being raised, someone giggled.

One of the madrichim – a survivor– walked over and slapped the boy.

Immediately, a Palestinian madrich came over and reprimanded the man.

"Never lay your hand on anyone again."

No one laid a hand on me, but I didn't care – I was going back to Rome.

Duni didn't believe me.

"They'll never let you go."

"I'm not asking permission, I'm just going."

"How will you get there?"

"I'll hitch a lift to Bergamo and get on a train. The Italian drivers always pick you up."

"They'll come after you."

"Let them come. I'm leaving tomorrow night after lights out."

"Okay, I'll come with you."

"You don't have to come, you like it here."

"I'm not staying without you."

"Neither am I."

Shimon had gotten into the act. Then another friend said he wasn't staying. The four of us decided to leave that night.

—

After walking for ten minutes on the highway, we saw a truck pull over and ran up to it. The driver rolled down the window.

"Where are you going?"

"Bergamo."

"Okay, hop in the back."

—

Sitting in the back of the truck, I have a feeling of freedom. As we bump down the winding road, I can smell pine trees and see the stars through a small window. But after ten or fifteen minutes, I see something brighter – the headlights of another vehicle, which passes us.

We stop and pull over.

After a few seconds, the back door opens.

Two madrichim, Polish survivors, are standing there. When they see us, their eyes light up. One of them addresses the driver in broken Italian.

"These kids have run away from home. We've come to take them back."

"Okay, make it snappy. I'm already behind."

One madrich looks at me as if he knows I'm the leader.

"Get out."

My friends climb out of the truck.

I'm in no hurry.

It takes me so long that the driver becomes impatient. He gets out of the cab and comes around to the back.

"What's going on?"

He takes one look at me and figures it out.

"Do you want to go back with these guys?"

I shake my head.

He looks at my friends.

They shake their heads.

"We're scared of them."

"Get back in the truck."

My friends climb back into the truck.

The driver turns to the madrichim.

"These kids don't want to come with you. They're coming with me."

"Let us talk to them."

"Talk to them all you want. But you'll have to do it on the way to Bergamo. I've wasted too much time on your family quarrel."

The truck driver climbs back into the cab. As the truck pulls away, the madrichim jump on the back.

They try to intimidate us, but it doesn't work. The farther we get from the kibbutz, the less chance they have of bringing us back. And since they've also hitch-hiked, they don't really feel like trying. They look at each other and shake their heads.

"I guess we'll have to let them go."

One of them yells to the driver.

"Stop the truck, we're getting off."

The truck stops and the madrichim get off.

As the truck starts moving again, we all heave a sigh of relief.

—

We stayed overnight at a transit camp in Bergamo, then boarded the train to Milan. In post-war Italy we didn't need tickets to travel by train. When the conductor came around, we just said "survivors" and rolled up our sleeves. The trip was short, but when we got off the train, everything was different. Milan wasn't an ancient city like Rome but an industrial centre with beautiful modern buildings. The headquarters of the Jewish Congress was in the *Villa Union*, an enormous glass-enclosed structure like a modern shopping mall. Today, every city in the world has one of these plazas, but to us, in 1947, it was breathtaking.

We saw the treasurer of the Congress and told him we wanted to go to Rome.

No problem.

The next day he gave us the tickets.

The leaders of the kibbutz were not happy to see us.

"You've made a mistake. There's nothing for you in Grotto Ferrata; all the children are in Silvano."

They wanted us to go back, but since we refused, they sent us to Grotto Ferrata. We spent the next few months bumming around Rome, visiting the Coliseum and seeing the sights. I loved Rome. It's a beautiful city and the people were warm and friendly. But the adults in the kibbutz didn't like to see us wasting our time. They didn't know what to do with us. When a fresh group of chayalim arrived from Palestine, the adults dropped the problem into their lap at the first meeting.

"These are the four boys," the kibbutz leader said, pointing us out.

There was the usual discussion. Some wanted to send us back to Silvano; others thought it was wrong to force us to go against our will. The final decision was a compromise.

"You have to go to a children's home, but we won't send you back to Silvano. We'll send you to Avigliano. Maybe it will suit you better."

Avigliano is a picturesque little town between Rome and Milan. The kinderhaim was in a beautiful old church that had been partially destroyed during the war and rebuilt with money from United Nations Relief and Rehabilitation Agency. It did suit us better. There were about one hundred of us, all over the age of sixteen, and our teachers, who were mostly chayalim, didn't treat us like children but like young men. They emphasized physical fitness and occupational training rather than academics. Every morning before class we did fifteen minutes of callisthenics.

Now that I was being treated as if I had some worth, I had no trouble paying attention or applying myself. I built myself up physically, learned to speak fluent Hebrew, and picked up mathematics, geography, and all the other subjects you normally take in school. Avigliano is where I finally got the education that I had missed as a child.

When we were asked what kind of trade we were interested in, I chose agriculture, as did most of the others. Agriculture is what a *chalutz* (pioneer) needed to know – our dream was to turn the desert into a garden. But first we had to get to the Holy Land. We were all waiting for aliyat bet. As soon as a boat was ready for us, we would travel to the port city of Genoa and depart for Palestine. We were ready to go at a moment's notice.

The notice never came, so we went on with our lives.

We were separated into four *kvutzas* (groups) and every *kvutza* had a leader. It was a temporary position and we all took turns at it. When it was your turn to lead, you led. And when it was your turn to mop the floor, you mopped the floor – even if you were a madrich. Every member of the kibbutz was equal to every other member, no matter what job he was assigned to. "*From each according to his ability, to each according to his need*," was the motto. We were taught that the desires of the individual are subservient to the good of the group. It's not an easy lesson to learn.

As soon as I arrive, every item I have acquired during my Roman holiday is confiscated.

"Turn everything in to the machzan (collective warehouse)."

The madrich accompanies me.

"Your suitcase too."

"What about my clothes?"

"Everyone's going to use them."

"What will I wear?"

"Don't worry, the person in charge of the machzan will find something to fit you. You can only wear one pair of pants."

For the first time in my life, I had nice clothes. I wasn't too happy to give them away, but I had no choice.

"Okay."

The madrich rolls his eyes and talks to himself out loud.

"This guy's going to be a problem!"

He's right. The next day, I see someone walking around in one of my new shirts.

"That's mine," I say, going up to him. "Take it off."

He looks at me like I'm crazy.

I rip it off his back.

—

The madrichim were very understanding. They tried to reason with me:

"When you don't have the necessities of life, Yakov, it's natural to be possessive of the few luxuries you can afford. But you have to get over that feeling, it's unhealthy. The kibbutz is your family and you have to share. You can only wear one shirt at a time."

"But this is a shmata (rag) and that's a new shirt. Why can't I wear it?"

"Because it belongs to the kibbutz. Maybe someone will join who has even nicer clothes than you. And they'll end up wearing them. When you're part of a kibbutz, you gain some things and you lose some things – the important thing is not to place so much importance on material possessions. It's too late for the older survivors to learn this – they're too set in their ways – but you have your whole life ahead of you. When you get to Eretz Yisroel, you'll have more important things to do than worry about wearing fancy clothes. You'll live on the kibbutz and wear what everybody else wears. You'll have your duties, just like everybody else, and if the kibbutz makes money it will be shared equally, no matter what job you do. This is the only way the kibbutz will survive. And it's the only way to build a new homeland from a desert."

⌒

Their talk went in one ear and out the other. The next day I saw another guy wearing my clothes and I confronted him.

"Why are you wearing that shirt?"

"Why shouldn't I wear it?"

"I'll show you why."

I beat the hell out of him. He was bigger than I was, so I didn't feel I had anything to apologize for.

The madrichim didn't see it that way. They called a meeting to discuss the problem.

The European-born madrichim wanted to send me back to Rome, but the chayalim were willing to give me another chance. One in particular stood up for me.

"We can't throw him out. It's not his fault."

"So whose fault is it, the guy he beat up?"

"It's Hitler's fault. You think you can undo the damage that was done in camps, overnight? We have to keep working with Yakov."

"There's nothing to work with – he won't listen to anyone. He's sixteen years old and wants things his own way. Every time he sees someone wearing a nice shirt, we're going to have another broken nose. This can't go on. We can't sacrifice the whole kibbutz for one individual."

My supporter gets an idea.

"Yakov, wait outside."

I go out of the room.

A few minutes later, he calls me back and asks me a question.

"How would you like to run the machzan?"

I look at him like he's lost his mind.

"What do you mean run it?"

"You'll be in charge. You can take whatever you want and give everyone else what you think they need. Would you be willing to do that?"

"Okay," I say in a tone that implies I'm doing him a favour.

—

I became boss of the machzan the very next day, and it was up to me to decide what my fellow kibbutzniks wore. "What size are you?" I'd ask, and see what I had to fit them. If you were a friend, you got nice clothes. If I didn't like you, you got some *shmata*. For the first time in my life I'd been give some authority, and I was drunk with power.

But I sobered up quickly. The novelty wore off. Before long, running the machzan became a job, not an indulgence and I stopped acting like a big shot. I gave people whatever clothes fit them, without paying any attention to who they were. I was more concerned with reorganizing the machzan. My predecessor had left a mess, which I spent hours cleaning up. Then I put in a system and made the machzan run like clock-work. It was so neat, you could eat off the floor. The

Soccer team

Gardening

Purim

madrichim were so impressed with my work that they made me head of my *kvutzah*.

I had big shoes to fill. Duni, who had been head before me, had done a terrific job. People didn't mind taking orders from him because he was such a nice guy. He didn't have a mean bone in his body. He later became head of all four *kvutzahs* and did a good job at that too.

I enjoyed being head of the *kvutzah* and worked hard at the job, but I didn't have Duni's *chaine*. Or patience. The worst part was waking people up in the morning. Getting everyone to the dining hall for flag raising was my responsibility, and I had to literally drag some guys out of bed. "Get away," they would yell and pull the covers over their head.

If you tried to pull the covers off, they put up a fight.

One guy hit me so hard that I lost my temper and gave him a shot that made his nose bleed. He became very upset. The madrichim called another meeting.

"I don't want the job of getting people up," I told them.

"All right," they said. "You'll just look after the machzan."

So the burden was removed from my shoulders.

This experience taught me that I was not cut out to be a leader. I already knew that I was not cut out to be a follower. I didn't like bossing people around or *being* bossed around. When I was given a job to do – whether it was cutting weeds, making barrels, or bending iron – I did it to the best of my ability without any prodding. To me, running the machzan was the ideal job. No one was looking over my shoulder, and I could indulge my weakness for nice things to my heart's content. I didn't know that this weakness was about to change the course of my life.

—

For the next eight months, apart from the occasional scrape, my life on the kibbutz was very pleasant. I spent most of the time studying, but I also enjoyed the singing, dancing, sports, and other recreational activities. A beautiful Russian girl named Bella became my first girlfriend. Many of the boys and girls paired up. This wasn't an Eastern European *shtetl* (village) but a secular Jewish community where mixing with the opposite sex was encouraged rather than forbidden. The madrichim openly discussed the facts of life but couples were discouraged from "going all the way." The new homeland would need children.

But *premature* pregnancy would not be a blessing. It wasn't easy for healthy sixteen-year-olds to exercise such self-control so we worked off our excess energy on the soccer field.

My friends and I played soccer for hours on end. Most of the time we played against each other because we couldn't find anyone else to play. We knew we were good, but we didn't realize *how* good until we played against an Italian men's team and beat them 1–0. This hand-picked team, with their professional coach, nice uniforms, and fancy boots, couldn't believe that they'd been beaten by a bunch of teenage DPs

That's what a few months on the kibbutz had done for us. I have a photograph of our soccer team, and you would never believe the healthy-looking young men in the picture are Holocaust survivors. Most of them are *smiling*. This is the only photograph I still have from that time. I took it with a camera I bought in Milan. Where did I get the money for a camera? From my "partner."

My weakness for nice things had caused me to bite the hand that fed me. I was running the machzan for the kibbutz, but I had also gone into business for myself.

OUTCAST

We lived an insulated life in the kinderhaim. It was an island of Jewish idealists surrounded by a sea of Italian realists. Contact with the outside world was kept to a minimum. When you are trying to instill the principles of collective living in young minds, *la dolce vita* (the sweet life) can be a distraction. A kibbutz had to be self-contained and self-sufficient. "When you are living on a collective farm in the Negev," we were told, "you can't pick up the telephone and call a plumber every time the toilet gets stopped up."

But we weren't living in the Palestinian desert; we were a stone's throw from a modern industrial city. When our toilets broke down, we called Milan for a plumber. When we needed toilet paper, it was delivered by truck. Tradesmen were coming and going all the time while I was running the machzan. One delivery man (a good-looking young Italian with shiny black hair who liked to drink) visited me almost every day.

My Italian was pretty good, but my new friend wasn't interested in conversation. There was a shortage of everything in post-war Italy, and I was sitting on a warehouse of goods. My Italian friend would wander around the machzan like a kid in a candy store. "You have such beautiful stuff here," he would say, feeling a blanket or a sheet. Then he'd smile, showing me his white teeth, and say what was really on his mind. "You could get a fortune for this stuff in Milano."

One day, he folds up a blanket and makes me a proposition.

"Let me take this. I'll give you lire."

He pulls some bills out of his pocket and holds them out.

I don't reach for them.

"What do I need with lire? I can't buy anything in here."

"Don't they let you go into town?"

"On weekends. But I'm not selling it to you."

"So give me a present. For my mother, she's a poor widow."

"I don't think I should do it."

But he already has it under his coat.

He folds up the lire and leaves them on the counter.

After that, my Italian friend took "a little present for his mother" every few days. I didn't like the idea of being a thief – I had never stolen a thing in my life, apart from food – but it was no big deal, just a shirt here and a pair of socks there – whatever would fit under his coat without making a bulge. Then one day my "friend" showed up with a suitcase.

"Are you crazy? You're going to get me caught! The madrichim are just looking for an excuse to toss me out. What if they ask you to open your suitcase?"

My partner in crime is very insulted by the suggestion that he would betray me. No Jewish Holocaust survivor was going to make him open his suitcase.

"Me Italiano!"

So I give him sheets, I give him clothing, and I have pockets full of lire.

Over the next few months, I spent money like a drunken sailor. Every weekend I'd go into town with my friends and we'd go to restaurants, have pictures taken, and have a wonderful time. I'd always buy something for Bella, who was living in a refugee camp with her parents. I had a wonderful girlfriend, money to spend, and I was working hard on my studies. Life was good. I knew that a Romanian madrich named Silica, who hated my guts, was keeping his eye on me, but I didn't give a damn. I was a cocky teenage kid sitting on top of the world.

Then, one night, Silica became suspicious. He stopped my partner in crime and made him open his suitcase. "How did you get this stuff?" Silica asked.

Signor "Me Italiano" sang like a bird!

—

The other madrichim wanted to wait until morning to deal with the situation, but Silica talked them into holding a meeting immediately. Now that he had caught me red-handed, he didn't want me to wiggle off the hook– by morning, the shock would have worn off and my crime might not seem so serious. They called a meeting of the entire kibbutz. They had to get Duni out of bed.

"What's going on?"

"Wake everybody up. Tell them to assemble for a discussion."

"Now?"

"Yes, right now."

When Duni and the others from my kvutza came into the dining hall, the madrichim were standing around with long faces – except for Silica, who was licking his lips. I couldn't even look at my friends. As I waited for the meeting to start, I wondered what my punishment would be. I knew they were going to make an example of me and, frankly, I didn't care. So they send me to jail. Big deal. After the slave labour camps, the thought of an Italian jail didn't scare me.

But listening to the head madrich recite my crimes in front of the entire kibbutz killed me.

I sit there, staring at the floor, as a man who has defended me in the past describes how I sold everyone's clothes, sheets, and blankets and put the money in my pocket.

Then Silica stands up and makes a speech.

"We did everything for this man and this is how he repays us!"

He's not the only one who speaks against me. I have made more enemies than friends.

The madrichim don't bother to take a vote; they decide among themselves and Silica delivers the verdict.

"Pack your suitcase, Weiss."

—

Bella met me at the train station. Facing her was even harder than facing my friends. When I boarded the train, she was crying.

"What's going to happen to you, Yakov?"

"I don't know."

"Write to me as soon as you get to Milano."

"Okay, I will."

The madrichim had given me a letter to give to the head of the Jewish Agency in Milan. It wasn't sealed. As soon as the train pulled out, I read it. Maybe they had *wanted* me to read it – otherwise why not seal it? The letter described my crimes in detail and said the kinderhaim did not have the facilities to handle me. *This boy needs special treatment.*

I didn't know what the "special treatment" would be nor did I care – as long as it wasn't physical. I was afraid of having the hell beaten out of me. There were some pretty tough people at the transit camp.

—

The head of the Jewish committee was sitting at a desk littered with paper. He was a Polish survivor and he spoke to me in Yiddish.

"Nu. What can I do for you, young man?"

I handed him the letter.

He reads it and his smile fades.

He sits there for a long time with a sad look on his face.

Then he gets up, comes around the desk, and puts his arm around me.

"You did a lot of bad things but they had no right to throw you out. You're only sixteen. Do you want to go back?"

"Never!"

He nods, sighs, and shakes his head.

"Yes, I can understand. But I don't know where to send you."

He thinks about it.

"Look, stay with me for a few days and I'll see what I can do for you."

That night I slept in his office. Or tried to sleep. People were coming and going outside the door all night. I started browsing through the things in the desk. In one drawer I found a box of money. Not a strongbox but an ordinary cigar box full of American currency. My landlord must have been collecting for some Zionist organization. When he arrived at the office the next morning, everything was just as he had left it.

"Did you sleep well?"

"Not too good. There was too much going on outside. You should lock your desk drawers." I tell him about finding the box of money.

"Did you take any?"

"No."

"Okay."

He doesn't bother to check the box – even though the letter from kibbutz has branded me a thief. He is more concerned about my welfare than my honesty.

"Go out and have something to eat. Then you can walk around the camp for a while. Maybe you'll find someone you know. Come back here after lunch."

There were hundreds of people in the transit camp, all headed for different locations throughout Italy. I mingled with them and tried to pick up information. I overheard some kids my age talking about going to Canada, but just as I was going to ask them what that was all about, I heard a familiar voice call out to me.

"E-E-Erno...."

I turned around to see Bercu Roth and his wife, Sarah. In addition to their son, who was a toddler, she was carrying an infant.

"Bercu!"

When my father's old helper saw me, his eyes filled with tears. He ran over and gave me a hug that almost broke my ribs.

"W-what are you d-doing here?"

I tell him the whole story, but not the real reason I left the kinderhaim.

Then he brings me up to date. He and Sarah, who have a new son, have just arrived from Germany.

"We're going to Palestine."

"Aliyah bet?"

"How else?"

"You'll have to wait."

"So we'll w-wait. I've got a job. I'm going to be a cook at the c-camp in F-Fermo. We're on our way there now. W-What are your p-plans?"

"I don't have any. I just know I don't want to live on a kibbutz. I've heard there are some kids going to Canada. Do you know anything about it?"

Yes, he'd heard about it. The Canadian Jewish Congress had convinced the government to modify its "none is too many" policy and take one hundred children that the Congress would sponsor. The children had to be between twelve and eighteen years old and in perfect health.

"T-They are r-registering over there," Bercu said, and he pointed to a long line of kids about my age. I made up my mind on the spot.

Bercu, a Zionist, was not happy about my decision and tried to talk me out of it.

"But you're waiting for aliyah bet."

"Not anymore. They kicked me out, remember?"

"So you'll join another kibbutz – one that's not so strict."

"I don't want to join a kibbutz. I want to go to Canada."

"You don't want to go to Eretz Yisroel?"

"No."

"Don't be so quick to answer; this is a big decision. Why don't you think it over for a day or two?"

In a day or two, the quota would be filled!

"I don't have to think it over; I want to register for Canada."

Bercu could see that he was wasting his breath. Suddenly he wasn't so friendly. "Do what you want," he said, going back to his paperwork. "Just make sure you let me know."

There were about fifteen kids ahead of me in the line, which led up a short flight of stairs to a door. It was a slow process. One kid would go in the door and come out ten or fifteen minutes later, and we'd all move a few feet closer. While I was waiting in line, I saw Duni wandering around in the crowd.

I called out to him.

When he saw me, his face lit up. He rushed over.

"Duni, what are you doing here?"

"I came to be with you. Why are you standing in this line?"

"I'm registering for Canada."

He was shocked.

"What do you mean, what about aliyat bet?"

"You still think they would take me?"

"Yes, I do!"

The night before, the entire kibbutz had had a long discussion about me, and Duni had spoken in my defense. He said he knew me better than anyone, that we had grown up together, and that I had never stolen a thing in my life. He told them how poor I was as a kid; how I was the only one who never brought a lunch to school; that he had nice parents and older brothers to look out for him, but that I had no one; I had to look after myself, as well as my younger siblings.

"The madrichim realize they were wrong to believe that Italian thief. They're willing to give you another chance. All you have to do is tell them it wasn't your idea to steal that stuff and that you're sorry."

"But I'm not sorry. I'm glad this happened. Now I have a chance to go to Canada. I'm not like you, Duni; I can't live on a kibbutz. I'm sick to death of having a twenty-minute discussion every time I want to go to the bathroom. But the kinderhaim suits you. You should go back."

"No, I want to be with you."

"So get in line, we'll go to Canada together."

"No, no, I want to see Moshe; his wife just had a baby."

Duni started to cry. He had a good reason to go to Palestine: his older brother Moshe was already there with his new family.

"Look, Duni, you're my best friend but your family comes first. Go back to the kibbutz; I'm going to Canada."

"But why Canada? How do you know there will be Jewish people there?"

I didn't. I didn't know a thing about Canada. But anyplace was better than living in another camp. I was sick of depending on others and being treated like a child. I was seventeen years old and ready to take responsibility for my life. I wanted to start making my own decisions, earning my own money, and spending it any way I liked. My life had been a nightmare – both before and after the Holocaust – and I wanted to make a fresh start. Not in two years, or even two months, but immediately.

"You're right, Duni, maybe Canada won't be the Garden of Eden, but anything is better than living like this. If there's a boat leaving this miserable place, I want to be on it." I had reached the front of the line.

The door opened and a kid came out.

"It's my turn, Duni. Goodbye."

Duni hugs me, with tears rolling down his cheeks.

I hug him back.

As I climb the stairs to begin my adult life, I am crying like a baby.

The End of the Beginning

At the base of the Statue of Liberty, at the entrance to New York Harbour, there is a poem by the Jewish poet Emma Lazarus in which the "land of the free" invites the nations of wartorn Europe to "give me your tired, your poor...." If the Dominion of Canada had a similar message at its gates, it might read: "Only the self-supporting need apply." At the end of the war, W. L. Mackenzie King's Liberal government did not exactly welcome refugees with open arms. Jewish refugees, in particular, were repugnant to the Canadian WASP establishment. The last thing the country needed was an infestation of pushy, impoverished non-believers. At least the Indians knew their place. But if you gave the Jews a finger, they'd take the whole hand. As soon as they made a bit of money, they'd move into your neighbourhood and want to join your country club. When Fred Blair, then head of the Canadian immigration department, was asked how many Jewish Holocaust survivors he thought Canada should accept, he is reported to have made the "witty" reply: *None is too many*.

But after a few years, government policy had changed – slightly. Canada was an enormous country with vast natural resources and very few inhabitants. Not to take a single refugee off the hands of its wartorn allies would be scandalous. So the Canadian Jewish Congress had pressured the King government to modify its refugee policy from "none is too many" to: "Well, maybe a hundred teenagers."

The Jewish community was to be responsible for feeding, clothing, and housing the newcomers until they could earn their own living. There was no way these impoverished European orphans would become a financial burden on this wealthy country. Only the healthy and physically fit would be considered as immigrants. Otherwise, it was first come, first served.

The Congress social worker who was sent to do the screening was a tough woman named Ethel Ostry. She looked at my DP card then started to question me.

"So you want to go to Canada, Yakov?"

"Yes."

"Are you a good boy?"

"*Very* good."

"What do you know about Canada?"

"Just that it's cold."

She laughed. "It's colder than Italy, but not all the time. Where I live the winters are very cold, but the summers are warm."

"Where's that?"

"In a city called Winnipeg. Have you ever heard of it?"

I shook my head.

"It's right in the middle of the country. You're *sure* you want to go to Canada?"

"Yes."

"Do you like to read?"

I didn't want to lie to her – but I didn't want to ruin my chances either.

"Sometimes."

"What about sports?"

This was a better question.

"I play a lot of soccer. I'm pretty good."

"So there's no trouble with your lungs?"

I shook my head.

"That's good because you'll have to have a complete medical examination."

"Now?"

"No, it might be another month or six weeks. Where are you going to be staying?"

"I don't know."

"When you find out, make sure you let us know."
She handed me a card. "We have to know where to
find you. In the meantime, you can use this to live
on."

She opened her desk drawer, took some money out
of a box, and gave it to me. Around here, everyone
seemed to have money sitting in his or her desk.

—

Bercu was very disappointed to hear that I had registered for Canada.

"When do you leave?"

"I don't know, not for a month at least."

That cheered him up – he had a month to talk me
out of it.

"What are you going to do until then?"

"I don't know."

"Why don't you come to Fermo with us? You can
probably get a job in the camp."

It sounded good to me.

"Okay, what's the phone number?"

I wrote down the phone number on a piece of paper
and took it to Mrs. Ostry.

"I already have it," she said. "There are three other kids from Fermo who registered – Saul Spitz, Martin Shane, and Nick Munsch."

This was the first time I heard the names of the three boys who were to become my friends.

—

The transit camp at Fermo, thirty kilometres from Rome, was run by British soldiers. There was no shortage of jobs there, but I wanted to get one of the better ones. The British were planning to appoint some civilian policemen, and I wanted to apply. You had to be there in person to be selected so I waited. And waited.…

The day they finally got around to selecting the policemen, I was playing soccer.

Bercu came running out to the field to tell me.

But I got there too late and ended up working on a garbage truck.

Our living accommodations were not much better than in the ghetto – large buildings divided into separate units by canvas. I shared a "room" with Bercu's brother-in-law, Sanyi, and dozens of boxes.

Sanyi was hoarding American cigarettes.

"They're as good as American dollars," he kept saying.

"Dollars don't dry up," I kept answering. "Either smoke them or sell them; there's no room for them."

I hated the sight of those lousy cigarettes, but the demand for them was huge. I made friends with an older Hungarian D. P. who made a lot of money rolling cigarettes and selling them one at a time. He offered me a free sample.

"No thanks," I said. "I don't smoke."

"It's time you started," he said, lighting one up. "Here, take a drag.

I shook my head. "It will make me sick."

"Don't be a sissy. One drag won't kill you."

So I sucked in some smoke.

"It's awful," I said, coughing it out.

"Don't worry, you'll get used to it."

He had lit another one for himself, so I had to finish the one I was holding. I couldn't throw it away – cigarettes were his livelihood. After that, he insisted on giving me a free sample every day, even though I hated the taste.

"Keep it up, keep it up," he would say like a broken record, "you'll get used to it."

And I did. When I finally started earning a bit of money, I had something new to throw it away on.

—

I have fond memories of the summer of 1947. The weather was beautiful and life was good. I met some other kids who were waiting to go to Canada and we hung around together. Saul Spitz was from Hungary, Martin Shane was from Poland, and Nick Munsch was from Romania. Martin and Nick were bums like me, but Saul was quiet and well educated. There was a recreation room where the three of us went to kill time. Bercu was the cook so we ate well and when we got paid, my new friends and I would go into town and raise hell.

After we'd been in camp for about six weeks, the four of us were called into the office of the "mayor," a British officer. A telegram from the Jewish Congress had arrived. We were to go for chest X-rays.

An ambulance drove us to a small hospital in the mountains in the middle of the night. There was such a demand for the X-ray machine that the technicians, all survivors, were working around the clock. One of the technicians we saw that night ended up in Winnipeg, where he took X-rays of weddings instead of lungs – he became a photographer.

Our X-rays turned out fine.

After we'd been back in Fermo for a few weeks, my friends and I received another telegram. We were going to Kuglasco, a camp near Milan.

A few days later, our train tickets arrived and I had to say goodbye to Bercu.

It wasn't easy. He broke down completely.

"W-write as soon as you g-get to C-C-C-Canada."

"Yes, yes, I will."

As we drive away, Bercu and Sarah are standing at the gate, crying. Sarah, who is carrying the baby, takes his chubby little arm and waves goodbye.

I intended to write, but when I arrived in Canada, I didn't know where to send the letter, so Bercu and I lost track of each other for many years. The next time I saw the Roth family, their "baby" was wearing an Israeli army uniform and weighed over two hundred pounds.

—

We had to wait four hours for the train to arrive. Nick Munsch almost tore the station apart. He was a wild Romanian who couldn't sit still for a minute. He was always running around, playing jokes or hatching schemes. The Romanian Jews were among the last to be deported, and Nick had managed to stay out of the camps by forging false identification papers that were good enough to fool the Nazis.

He wasn't a typical survivor because there is no such thing. Every survivor has a different story. We've all been through hell, but we haven't all been in the camps. Just looking at our faces, you can't tell which of us has witnessed Hitler's "Final Solution" from inside the barbed wire. You have to look in our eyes.

Because we were to have a medical examination in Kuglasco, we had to stay overnight. It was a tiny camp that wasn't equipped for visitors. A rosy-cheeked little Hungarian who looked like Peter Lorre told us where to go.

"You can sleep in the storeroom."

In the storeroom, we found a bunch of mattresses piled one on top of another, and I pulled one down. But when the guy in charge of the camp – a good-looking Romanian with curly blond hair like Harpo Marx– came by, he was very upset.

"Who told you to touch that?"

"What do you want me to do, sleep on the floor?"

Harpo Marx and I almost got into a fight.

Peter Lorre broke it up.

"It's okay, Mickey. I told them to sleep here."

The peacemaker, Benny Blum, and the guy who got upset, Mickey Hoch, both ended up in Winnipeg, where we became friends.

Nick, Saul, Martin, and I all passed the medical and were sent for a week to Adriatica, where we slept on real beds. There were about one hundred people at the camp, which was run by a woman from Canada who held talks, describing the country and telling us what to expect when we got there. The Congress was responsible for finding us places to live and jobs.

"If you're lucky, you might get a Jewish family to sponsor you. Then you'll have a chance to complete your education."

(Some of the kids got lucky – my friends and I got jobs.)

After a week of orientation, we were given money, train tickets and a document with our picture on it.

"Keep this in a safe place. If you lose it, they won't let you on the boat."

I put my passport in my shirt pocket and buttoned it up. My back pocket was reserved for my wallet – which was stuffed with photographs of my friends in the kibbutz. When I boarded the train for the port city of Genoa, those pictures were all I had to remind me of my happy years in Italy.

At Sea

We arrived in Genoa at ten in the morning but weren't due to sail – on a Greek luxury liner – until six in the evening, so my friends and I took some time to see the city. We had breakfast at a waterfront café, then decided to go our separate ways.

"I'll meet you at the ship at five – the Nea Hellas, right?"

"Okay, I'll find it."

Genoa is a colourful city of canals, gondolas, fishing boats, and cargo ships from all over the world. The waterfront streets were jammed with sailors looking for a good time. It was like a carnival, with food stands, sideshows, and gambling games. I stopped to watch the Wheel of Fortune, which seemed to be a popular game.

People were pressing in on me from all sides.

"How does it work?" I asked a man standing beside me.

He explained the game – you put down some money and if the wheel stopped on your symbol, it paid three to one. After watching for a while, I decided to take a chance.

I put my hand in my pocket to take out some money. I'm carrying it loose because my wallet is stuffed with photographs of Bella and my friends on the kibbutz. It's so fat that it makes a bulge in my back pocket. I take out a few lire and am about to put them down when the man standing beside me says something.

"Don't play."

"Why?"

He nods at the man who is operating the wheel.

"He has a pedal. He can stop the wheel anywhere he wants."

I thanked him, put the money back, and pushed my way out of the crowd.

Later I stopped to watch a different gambling game. Then I moved on to a sideshow advertised by a big poster of a half-naked woman with a black beard. The sidewalk was so jammed I kept bumping into people. One of them was a girl who looked like Bella.

Saying goodbye to Bella had been so hard.

She couldn't stop crying. Why did I have to go?

Because I had nothing to stay for. I was sick of living in camps. Canada was a beautiful country. Why didn't she come with me?

She started to cry even harder.

"I can't leave my family, Yakov."

I didn't try to talk her out of it. Her father was a big-shot Communist. They were going back to the Soviet Union, and I would never see her again.

Suddenly I had an overwhelming urge to look at her picture.

I reached for my wallet.

I didn't feel anything – it was gone!

I found a restaurant, went to the washroom, and took off my pants in a toilet stall. My back pocket had been cut away, probably by a razor blade. I felt like I was going to throw up. All my pictures were gone.

What about my passport?

I unbuttoned my shirt pocket.

Thank God it was still there!

—

The *Nea Hellas* was a luxury liner, but my first ocean voyage was far from luxurious. I was seasick from the minute we left port. For the first time in my life, I refused food. And you never saw such food – they served us wine with breakfast – but I couldn't look at it. I tried to keep something down, but nothing would stay down. I kept eating and throwing up, eating and throwing up, all the way to Canada. In eleven days,

I went from one hundred and sixty pounds to one hundred and forty.

Weight wasn't all I lost on the trip to Canada. We were each given ten Canadian dollars in spending money when we boarded the ship. In 1947, ten dollars was real money. But on the first day out I got into a gin rummy game with Aaron Kozlovitch and Max Ludwig – two new bums I became friendly with – and they cleaned me out. I started my new life in Canada the same way I had spent most of my life in Europe – undernourished, penniless, and miserable.

PART TWO
CANADA
(1948–2001)

JACK WEISS, CANADIAN

When the *Nea Hellas* landed in Halifax, Nova Scotia, a number of people from the Jewish community were waiting to meet us. They had come in response to an ad in the local paper asking for volunteers to provide transportation and temporary accommodation. I was driven to the home of a young couple whose name, unfortunately, I don't remember. They didn't speak Yiddish, so we had a little trouble communicating. I stayed with them for a couple of days and they treated me like a son. I had my own room with a radio that I listened to for hours, trying to pick up a bit of English. The husband, who owned a shoe store, fitted me with a new pair of shoes and offered me a job.

"If you'd like to stay in Halifax, you can live with us and I'll teach you the shoe business."

I appreciated the offer, but I wasn't interested in settling down in the first place we came to. I wanted to see the country. So I thanked him but said I didn't want to leave my friends.

After a few days in Halifax, we resumed our journey. My first time on a North American train was an experience I'll never forget. Sailing west across the ocean I couldn't eat; travelling west across Canada I couldn't sleep. Our Pullman car was like a madhouse. All night my crazy friends would lie awake telling dirty jokes, yelling insults, or swinging from berth to berth like monkeys. During the day we'd play cards and get into arguments. I almost got into a fistfight when Aaron Kozlovitch accused me of cheating. Or maybe I accused him; I don't remember. I just remember I was in no mood for horseplay.

The ocean voyage had taken a lot out of me. I was homesick and heartsick. I couldn't stop thinking about Bella. Our chaperone from the Jewish Congress, Miss Lyons, had a problem with my name (she pronounced it "Wees") and even *that* bugged me.

Miss Lyons held meetings on the train to discuss our plans. Like Ethel Ostry, she was from Winnipeg, so I asked her about the city. She told me the same thing Ethel Ostry had: it was cold in winter and warm in summer. "But the people are always nice," she said with a smile.

I believed her. She was a very nice person.

I talked it over with my friends and twenty-six of us decided to go to Winnipeg.

Some of the others got off in Toronto.

I didn't get a chance to see Toronto, but I did spend a nice day in Montreal. We went to the YMHA (Young

Men's Hebrew Association), swam in the pool, had a steam bath, and ate in the kosher restaurant. Back on the train, I was in a much better mood. The last few days of the train trip were much more pleasant. By the time we pulled into the station in Winnipeg, Miss Lyons had even learned to pronounce my name correctly.

—

At the time of my arrival, Winnipeg was the third largest city in Canada. An overgrown farm town sitting in the middle of the country and surrounded by flat prairie, it was a city big in meatpacking, the grain trade, the fur trade, and the garment trade. Miss Lyons was right: the climate was cold but the people were warm. Winnipeg had the largest Jewish community in western Canada and we were welcomed with open arms. Those of us who weren't adopted by private families were looked after by the Canadian Jewish Congress. Its office was in the Confederation Building on Main Street, a stone's throw from the YMHA, which occupied a converted factory or warehouse on Albert Street, in the heart of the garment district.

Mr. Heinz Frank, the head of the Congress, was a wonderful man. He knew what was important to boys of our age and arranged for Churchill's – a big wholesale/retail dry goods store – to outfit us with new clothes. (The Churchill family adopted a young survivor who would eventually own the business.) "Ask for Mr. Skinner," Heinz Frank told us. "He'll look after you."

Mr. Skinner was a real character. He was full of jokes and didn't treat the six of us like *schnorers* (beggars) but like customers. He gave each of us a couple of white shirts then led us to the back of the wholesale area, where we saw racks and racks of suits. "Pick your own," he said and walked away.

It's like I'm back in the machzan, only better. We wander through the suits, feeling material and looking at price tags. The most expensive suit is a blue pinstripe. Aaron (who will soon change his last name to Kaye) decided to try one on.

"What do I look like?" he says, coming out of the change room.

"Like Al Capone," I say.

"I'll take this one," he tells Mr. Skinner.

The rest of us chose something else, but we were the exception. The next day it looked like the Y was hosting a gangster convention – there were half a dozen young Holocaust survivors wearing the same pinstripe suit.

Heinz Frank talked about getting us jobs.

"What about school?" I asked.

"That won't be easy," he said. "We don't have the money."

A few of the new arrivals were sponsored by local families, but most of us were boarding in private homes at Congress expense, so unless you were an outstanding student, you were expected to start earning a living as soon as possible.

Mr. Frank suggested that we learn a trade.

I had no objections. "I'd like to be a jeweller," I said.

"Why not a furrier?" he suggested. "In this country a furrier can always make a living."

It sounded good to me, and to eleven others.

Mr. Frank got the twelve of us jobs blocking skins at Neaman Fur. It was difficult and messy work. Someone would wet the skin and two of us would stretch it over a board and nail it down. Sometimes the skin would rip and an operator would have to sew it up, which would diminish its value. Even if it didn't rip, holding it in place while you hammered in the tacks wasn't easy. For every one time we hit the tack, we hit our finger twice. By the end of the first day, our hands were black and blue and our fingernails were filthy from the greasy skins. Some of the guys were ready to quit, but we cheered up when Sam Berg, our boss, gave us each a five-dollar bill.

"Just to tide you over."

It was not bad pay for a day's work. In those days, twenty-five dollars a week was an unheard-of salary for a novice. So I worked hard for the next four days, looking forward to payday. But when Percy, the foreman, handed me my envelope, it contained only three bills – a ten, a five, and a one. "Percy," I said, holding up the sixteen dollars, "what's this?"

"Money," he said. "When you work here you get paid."

All the workers laughed. They had all started at the bottom and knew that a stretcher was paid forty cents an hour, which is sixteen dollars for a forty-hour week. The five-dollar advance had been something extra that Mr. Berg had given us as a gesture.

"To hell with this," some of my friends said as we left the plant. They quit and went to work in the needle trade, where they could earn as much as twenty-four dollars a week. But I stayed at Neaman's, blocking skins. It was a lousy job, but if I wanted to learn the fur business I had to start somewhere.

Most of my first paycheques went for room and board. I was sharing a room with Saul Spitz in the North End of Winnipeg, which in those days was the heart of the city's Jewish community, as well as where most of the Ukrainians, Poles, and other "ethnic" types lived. The South End was reserved for the white Protestant establishment. Saul and I were living in an apartment above a drugstore on the corner of Inkster and Main, right across the street from Omnitsky's Kosher Butcher Shop.

Our landlords were the Trutes. Mr. Trute, head of the *Chesed Shel Emmes* (Jewish Burial Society), was a quiet older man who minded his own business. Mrs. Trute, his third wife, was a much younger woman who minded everyone's business but her own. She was the type of ignorant *yenta* who was always trying to impress you with her "Jewishness." I was anxious to learn English, but from the very first day she insisted that I speak to her in Yiddish.

"My Yiddish isn't too good," I told her. "My Hebrew is much better."

"So we'll talk Hebrew."

The next day, just to make conversation, I said to her in Hebrew, "I see there's a kosher butcher across the street."

"Don't address me in a Gentile tongue."

"I was speaking Hebrew," I said to her in Yiddish.

"I don't speak Hebrew."

Mrs. Trute reminded me of the relatives on my mother's side of the family – a vulgar hypocrite who pointed out everyone's faults and was blind to her own. Once she scolded me for referring to a Gentile girl I knew as a *shikseh* – which, like many Yiddish terms describing Gentiles, has a slightly derogatory connotation.

"It's not nice to call someone that."

So, from then on, I was careful to use the word *maidel* (young girl) regardless of whether the girl in question was Jewish or Gentile. It wasn't much of a problem because my social life was centered around the YMHA. Virtually all the girls I associated with were Jewish.

One of the girls took a liking to me and used to call me up – which was very unusual in those days. Every time she called, my landlady's ears perked up. Finally she couldn't stand it any longer.

"Who is this girl who keeps calling you?"

"Someone I know from the Y. Her name is Tzipi Rabinovitch."

Mrs. Trute doesn't believe me; a nice Jewish girl would never call up a boy.

"It must be a shikseh."

That was Mrs. Trute.

One day, my friend Aaron, who lived around the corner, dropped by to see me.

"Can we go into my room?" I asked Mrs. Trute.

"No visitors."

So Aaron and I had to stand outside the door, in the middle of winter, and talk. After a few minutes, I was freezing to death. "Maybe we should go to your place," I suggested.

"If I can't come to your room," Aaron said, "you can't come to mine!"

That was Aaron, may he rest in peace. You never knew what to expect from him. He came from a small Polish town near the Russian border and had escaped the Nazis by hiding in the forest with his father. But they got into an argument and his father, like my step-mother, chased him away. Fair-haired Aaron joined the Polish partisans. He was a good-looking kid who, like a mischievous child, was extremely lovable. When Aaron Kaye died, on December 29, 1992, I lost my closest friend.

—

I soon moved in with Mickey Hoch and Hymie Tagger, who were living with a Mr. and Mrs. Mazo in a house on Scotia Street. It was a nice house, right beside the Red River, but I no longer had my own room. I slept in a single bed in the baby's room. At least she was a good baby and didn't disturb me.

Mickey, who later became a successful garment manufacturer, was working in a cap factory, and Hymie was studying architecture at university. The Mazos were nice people and I got along with my new roommates, but I yearned for a little more privacy. As soon as I got the chance, I moved out of the Mazos' house and in with my future in-laws, the Victors.

GROWING UP

Apart from hanging around Mickey's Pool Room on Selkirk Avenue, the YMHA was my only social life. Every Saturday night the Y held a dance, and it was at one of these "canteens" that I saw a beautiful fair-haired girl I had never noticed before. "Who's that?" I asked Ruth Letinsky.

"Sue Victor. Do you want me to introduce you?"

What a question. It was love at first sight! Ruthy introduced me to her friend and we've been together ever since.

Suzy was in her last year of high school when we started dating. We'd walk from her house to Main Street for chips and a coke. In those days Kelekis restaurant sold shoestring potatoes in brown paper bags – five cents for a small; ten cents for a large. Sometimes we'd walk to the Derry Dell, on Salter Street, for an ice cream cone – five cents for a single; ten cents for a double. Later, I bought a 1939 Studebaker from some people who owned a fish and chips stand on Salter Street, not far from Suzy's house, and we would go for drives.

Jack and Sara, 1950

Sue lived on Pritchard Avenue, which wasn't exactly a slum, but it wasn't as nice as Scotia Street. Her parents owned a triplex; they lived in one unit and rented out the other two. Suzy was their oldest child – she had a younger sister and brother – and her parents were not thrilled with her choice of a boyfriend. I was not only a lousy catch; I was interfering with her studies too. Sue had been a top student until she started going out with me. A girl as beautiful and intelligent as their older daughter would have no trouble attracting a future doctor or lawyer. So what did she see in a greenhorn who worked in the fur trade? What was the big attraction? Finally Suzy's parents decided to see for themselves. "Invite him over for dinner," they said.

The Victors weren't well off, but they were very nice people and when they saw that I wasn't a wild Hungarian, but a serious, hard-working young man, they became reconciled to their daughter's choice. When the Victors moved out of the triplex into a single-family dwelling a few blocks away on Manitoba Avenue, they looked on me not only as an acceptable boyfriend but as a potential boarder.

"Y'know we have an empty room," Mrs. Victor would hint, every time I came over. Why should I pay forty-five dollars a month to share a room when I could have my own room for the same price? So I gave the Mazos notice and moved in with the Victors.

I was living under the same roof as the love of my life, but that was as close as I got to her. Her father watched us like a hawk. Mr. Victor was a fine old gentleman who worked in a tailor shop in Transcona, a satellite town on the east side of the Red River, about six miles from his front door. To save the price of transit fare – ten cents – he walked to work and back every day. Later, he moved to a shop on Broadway – only a three-mile walk. He didn't make much money as a tailor, but he gave every penny to his wife and they got by.

When Sue graduated from high school, she found a job in the classified ad department of the Winnipeg Free Press. I had worked my way up at Neaman Fur and was making twenty-five dollars a week, a good salary. So, after going together for about two years, I asked her to marry me.

She said yes.

—

Sara "Sue" Victor and I were married on June 4, 1950, in a ceremony at the I. L. Peretz School on Aberdeen and Salter. A few weeks before, we had been carrying sandbags with most of the other people who hadn't evacuated the city. I will always remember the year of my wedding as "the year of the flood."

Winnipeg sits at the junction of two rivers: the Red, which flows north from the United States, and the Assiniboine, which flows east from Saskatchewan. The two muddy rivers join at "the Forks," which is located at the site of Upper Fort Garry, a few blocks from Portage and Main. The swollen Red River then flows into Lake Winnipeg, a huge, muddy lake about eighty kilometres downstream. In winter, the rivers freeze solid, but at spring breakup they rise so suddenly that storm sewers are liable to back up and flood basements. Occasionally the spring runoff is so heavy that the rivers overflow their banks. That is what happened in the spring of 1950. The Victors' house was far enough away from the river to escape major damage, but people like the Mazos, who lived on Scotia Street, rode to their front doors in motorboats. I don't know if Mickey and Hymie were still living there at the time.

—

Shortly after we married, Sue and I moved out of her parents' house into an apartment on Burrows Avenue,

a few blocks farther north. In Winnipeg, the farther
you went from the centre of the city, the nicer the
neighbourhood. Burrows Avenue was a long way from
Scotia Street, but it was a step up from Manitoba
Avenue.

The owner, a young Jewish guy named Joe Kives,
became a friend of ours. We also became friends
with three other young couples who lived there,
the Greenfelds, the Ostroves, and the Friedmans.
At night, after work, we'd all get together and play
cards.

Suzy made a *mensch* out of me. The backward im-
migrant kid who couldn't get along with other people
was now a responsible adult with a wonderful wife, a
nice apartment, a "normal" social life, and a steady
job. The four years that Suzy and I lived in that apartment on Burrows were very happy times. We had
each other, we had friends; we had a new refrigerator.
There was just one thing missing....

On May 24, 1954, Sue gave birth to a healthy baby
boy whom we named *Shloime*, after my father. It's
traditional among Jewish people to name children
after deceased relatives, but it's the Hebrew name that

is passed from generation to generation. The closest English equivalent of *Shloime* is Solomon, but Suzy and I wanted a more Canadian name so we chose Stephen. Biblical names were out of fashion in 1954. (They're back in fashion now – my youngest grandson is named Joshua)

With the extra mouth to feed Suzy, and I could no longer afford the apartment. Today you can be a career woman and a mother at the same time, but in the 1950s you had to make a choice – you were either a "two-income family" or a real family. Suzy quit her job and we moved back in with her parents.

A little more than a year later, on September 10, 1955, our son Jerry was born.

The Weiss family was complete.

Although we had fewer expenses and built-in baby-sitters, I wasn't comfortable living with my in-laws. They were lovely people, but I wanted to provide for my own family. So while the kids were still infants, the four of us moved back into a place of our own.

For a while things were tough, but gradually they improved. While others in the fur industry were laid off from time to time, I never went without work.

The services of a reliable, conscientious, and skilful worker are always in demand. A man I knew named Rombom opened a small fur shop on Selkirk Avenue and offered me a job. I went to work for him and he paid me well.

Meanwhile, the boys were growing up. When they were old enough to go to school, Suzy went back to work as executive secretary at their Hebrew day school. Sue never had to look for another job. She has excellent secretarial skills and enjoys dealing with people. Working at the Talmud Torah was a demanding job, but she loved it.

I was good at sewing muskrat skins together, but I wasn't in love with it. I was tired of being an employee. I wanted to go into business for myself, but the only other thing I was qualified to do was drive a car. So I took the few dollars we had saved up and bought a cab – as usual, "on time."

Once you had a licence, you had to work with one of the three cab companies in town: United, Veteran's Nash, or Duffy's. They were all independent companies, which meant drivers paid a weekly fee (about fifteen dollars) for the use of the company name and dispatch facilities.

I started out with United but soon switched to Duffy's, which had more than sixty taxis. The city was divided into areas and the closest taxi took the call. Drivers who were caught "jumping the line," were fined. The drivers elected inspectors to ensure that everyone followed the rules.

Driving a cab was a tough way to make a living – you had to be lucky to survive. If you had car trouble, your income stopped but your expenses continued. In addition to weekly payments to Duffy's and monthly payments on the car, I had to pay my own maintenance and repairs. I worked fourteen-hour shifts, leaving the house early in the morning and coming back at nine or ten at night.

Luckily I found the job interesting. I enjoyed driving and meeting people. The only thing that annoyed me was when once in a while a passenger would notice my concentration camp number and ask what it was. I sometimes explained what it was even though I didn't like to talk about it. As time went on, I kept thinking about having the tattoo removed. I even went as far as discussing this with my doctor.

OLD SCARS, NEW WOUNDS

When are you going to let me take that off?
Dr. Peikoff asked me the same question
about my tattoo every time I came to his office. And I
always gave him the same answer.

"I'll think about it."

The late Sam Peikoff was the kind of doctor you
don't see anymore – one who treated you like a person rather than a source of income. He'd become one
of Winnipeg's busiest Jewish practitioners, but as a
young man, he'd practised in rural Manitoba, where
he did everything from removing appendixes, to de-
livering babies, to pulling teeth, and he still had the
ways of a country doctor. Dr. Peikoff loved to talk. He
would look at the faint blue numbers on my forearm
and say, "let me take it off."

"I can do it so you won't even know it was there."

"I don't think I should."

"Do you need it to remind you?"

That was the last thing I needed. I agreed to have
my tattoo removed the next morning.

It was time to look for another line of work.

—

Every day for the next few months, I scanned the classified pages of both daily newspapers. There were a lot of jobs advertised but few that appealed to me – and I wasn't qualified for any of the good ones. Then one day I saw an ad for transit drivers. Winnipeg Transit was the public utility that operated all the streetcars and buses in town. Getting hired as a Transit driver was like getting hired by the post office – you had a job for life.

I went to the Winnipeg Transit offices and filled out an application. Two weeks later, I was called in to take an aptitude test, which I passed. After six weeks of training at half pay, I had to take final tests and I was finally hired at full pay.

I drove for Winnipeg Transit for six months but found the split shifts very stressful. I handed in my notice.

I resumed driving my taxi. By this time, I was almost thirty-nine years old and had teenage children in high school and I wanted to better myself. I sold my taxi and started looking for another business.

After looking for a few months, I found a business that appealed to me, even though it was seasonal. I felt I could handle it. There was also a rental property behind the store with five apartments that brought in extra income.

The people who sold me the business were very considerate and taught me the operation of the ice cream store, including how to make my own simple syrups and toppings.

They told us that they had one lady who came in every day to help and at the height of the season they hired eight additional helpers. It sounded good! I even had our two sons working for me and my wife did the payroll and the deposits. Even though I had lots of responsibilities and work – cleaning the machines daily, making syrup, filling the hoppers and ordering supplies – I loved my new venture. I was even able to take a trip the odd winter. I consider the years in the ice cream store as happy ones. I was in the ice cream store six years and sold it for a small profit.

—

I now had money to invest, and when you have money to invest word gets around. A man named Shoznitzer – a former Israeli who had married a Winnipeg girl – approached me with a proposition. The St. Vital

Hotel was for sale and he wanted me to buy it along with him and his brother-in-law.

—

The St. Vital was a medium-size suburban hotel that catered to the younger crowd. The rooms brought in a few dollars, but if there was any money to be made, it was going to come from the beverage room. We let the managers go and each of us took a shift so that one of us would be there at all times. This way, we could make it go and pay the mortgage, which was substantial.

—

What we later discovered, is that a small hotel owner couldn't make money unless he owned one of those low-rent flophouses with a liquor licence on the Main Street strip. Otherwise, the overhead would kill you – especially in the 1960s and 1970s, when every suburban hotel had to have *live* entertainment to attract customers. The few dollars we made in the pub went into the pockets of the bands. Then the Manitoba government passed a law that forced all beverage rooms to close between 6 p.m. and 7 p.m. so that

Jack, bus driver

regular patrons would go home for dinner with their families.

Our customers didn't go home – they went across the street to the Canadian Legion, which was a private organization that didn't have to close. Once a beer drinker sits down, he doesn't like to get up again. After the "curfew" you could have shot off a cannon in our pub without hitting anyone but Shoznitzer or me. We were working like horses and taking home peanuts.

A short time later, we sold the St. Vital Hotel. We each lost twelve thousand dollars but we considered ourselves lucky just to get out. My adventure in the hotel business was over. I decided to go back to something with a little more security – if they would have me.

—

It had been fourteen years, but Mr. Lalonde at the Winnipeg Transit remembered me.

I was retrained, retested, rehired, and before long I had my own run. Times had changed. More people were retiring so runs became available more quickly, but driving a bus was still a stressful job – especially in winter, when road conditions are hazardous. I drove a Winnipeg Transit bus from 1977 to 1984 and received several safety awards for accident-free driving. Those seven years of bus driving were hard but not as hard on me emotionally as my two-week "vacation" in Israel.

Belated Aliyah

In 1946, when I was sixteen years old, I began a journey to the Jewish homeland. In 1980, I finally made it there. To celebrate my fiftieth birthday, Suzy and I signed up for a two-week tour of Israel. The tour director told us that for the first week we would travel in a group during the day and be on our own in the evenings. After that we would have another week to relax and look up family and friends.

The first week there we didn't have time to breathe, let alone look up anybody. Israel is a tiny country – you can drive from one end to the other in a single day – but there's a lot to see. We stayed in a fancy hotel in Tel Aviv, which is a modern city, but we didn't get a chance to enjoy it. A bus picked us up at six in the morning and didn't drop us off until seven at night, by which time we were too exhausted to do anything but eat dinner and go to bed. As we travelled around by bus, our guide – a *Sabra* (native Palestinian) who had been a colonel during the Six Day War – pointed out bombed-out tanks and trucks that had been left beside the road as memorials. He told us who had died

Hometown memorial plaque

at each site, where they were attacked – it was a history lesson you couldn't learn from a book.

Israel has thousands of years of history, and every inch of land is soaked in blood: Jewish blood, Arab Blood, Christian Blood, pagan blood – a highlight of the tour was Massada, the hilltop fortress that King Herod built during the Roman occupation. It was a cold day and a long climb. At the top, we could see for miles. This was where the Children of Israel had committed suicide rather than surrender to the Roman army.

I picked up a few stones to take home, but our guide told me to put them back. "If everyone who comes up here takes away a stone," he explained, "eventually they could carry away the mountain."

At the end of the sightseeing tour, I had one week to look up my friends. I started making inquiries, stopping people on the street and asking them questions. Over the years I had lost most of my Hebrew, but I had also lost my inhibitions. I talked to perfect strangers as if I'd known them all my life. Israel was not a foreign country to me; the minute I stepped off the plane I felt at home. Eventually word got around that a tourist was asking about Beregszasz, and someone came to the hotel to see me.

"There's an old man just down the street who's from there," the visitor told me.

The old man was not too helpful. "I've been here since 1939," he said. "Everyone I knew is gone. We have a *yurtzeit* (memorial service) in May. People come from all over."

"People originally from Beregszasz?"

"Where else? We have an organization."

I took out a pen and a pad. "Can you give me the names of any of the members?"

"What do I know from names? We have a president, he keeps a list."

"Who is your president?"

He tries to remember, but can't come up with a name.

"Wait, I know who can help you. We have a member, a very nice guy, Csopy Klein. He owns Rococo."

I had heard of Rococo – an Israeli ticket agency for performers from all over the world – but I'd never heard a name like Csopy.

"It's a nickname," the old man said. "It means … you know, *klein*."

"Small?"

"Yes, what's the word they use for a small guy?"

"Shorty?"

"That's it, Shorty Klein!"

The old man gave me Shorty's` telephone number and as soon as I got back to the hotel I called him.

"Sure, I know who the president is," Shorty Klein said. "Citrom Yankle."

"Oy vay!"

Klein laughed. "You know him?"

"Know him? My father was ready to kill him!"

"How come?"

Jacob Citrom was the head of the relief committee who refused to give my father money to buy me shoes when I was walking around in rubber boots with no socks. He was the kind of religious hypocrite that made my blood boil. But I wasn't going to let that spoil my chances of getting the names and addresses of my old friends.

"It doesn't matter, it was a long time ago. Can we go see him?"

"Sure, I'll take you tomorrow. There's only one problem, tomorrow is Saturday...."

"And if he sees us drive up in a car, he won't let us in the house."

"You do know him, all right," Klein said with a laugh. "I'll park a block away from the house. He should be home from the synagogue by noon. I'll be at the hotel around one, okay?"

"Fine."

"Okay, wait for me in the lobby."

"How will I know who you are?"

"Don't worry, you will."

Next day, at the appointed time, Sue and I were standing in the lobby, watching people come and go. Trying to spot Klein was like trying to pick out a single car on Portage and Main during rush hour. How was I going to recognize a perfect stranger in this crowd? And then suddenly I see him looking for me. "Shorty" Klein would stick out in any crowd; he was a head taller than everyone else in the lobby!

A woman about our age was with him. "This is my wife, Eva," he said as we introduced ourselves. Eva Klein was Hungarian too, but not from Beregszasz. Csopy was a few years older than I, and he didn't remember me.

"I remember your father used to have a bakery."

"Yes, but he lost it."

"Have you eaten lunch yet?"

"I'm not hungry."

"We can go to a restaurant. We have plenty of time.…"

"No, I'm okay, let's just go."

Csopy knew how I felt. I wasn't the first survivor who'd come to Israel, asking about Beregszasz. "I'll bet your stomach's been turning over since you talked to me last night," he said as we went outside.

His car, an older Mercedes Benz, was double-parked in front of the hotel. Half the cars on the street – including cabs – were Mercedes Benz or BMW. West Germany was one of the few industrial nations that had trade relations with Israel, so Hitler's victims were now driving German cars. We drove close to our destination.

He pulled onto a side street and we walked one block to a modern building, where Citrom Yankle had a condo.

Klein knocked on the door.

Citrom Yankle opened it.

His hair was grey and he had a longer beard; otherwise, he hadn't changed.

"I think I remember you," he said, closing the door behind us.

He invites us to sit down and takes out a list of names.

"Who do you want to find?"

"Duni Yakobovics, Bercu Roth ..." I mention a few other names.

He puts on his reading glasses and looks at the list. He's having a hard time seeing in the dim apartment but because it's the Sabbath he can't turn on a light until sundown.

Finally he finds the names of my friends.

I write down their addresses and phone numbers.

Citrom Yankle puts away the list.

"You'll stay for tea?"

His offer to feed me is thirty-five years late, but it would be impolite to refuse, so we have tea and pastry.

I manage to drink my tea and eat my egg cookie without choking.

As soon as we're back in the car, Eva extends another invitation.

"I'd like you to come to our place."

—

We spent the rest of the day with the Kleins, who wined and dined us and chauffeured us around Tel Aviv. They couldn't do enough for Suzy and me. Csopy and Eva loved Suzy. Everybody loves Suzy, but they seemed to like me too. When they drove us back to the hotel, we invited them up to our room. We sat and talked until I could hardly keep my eyes open. This couple we had just met a few hours ago were

Childhood friends, Israel 1980

already like old friends. "Keep in touch," Csopy said when they finally got up to go.

"I will."

I started to undress as soon as the door closed behind them.

I fell into bed and slept like a stone.

—

Next morning I woke up early so I could start looking for my friends.

Bercu was first on my list.

"He lives on Pinchas Street," I said to Suzy. "We'll have to take a taxi."

"Don't you think you should phone first?"

"I wouldn't know what to say."

"But what if he's not home?"

"If he's not home, he's not home. I can't phone."

As I walk into Bercu's building, my heart is pounding like a hammer. I see an older man coming down the stairs and recognize him immediately.

"Bercu."

He stops and looks at me – he has no idea who I am.

"It's Erno."

His mouth falls open.

"Erno?"

Bercu runs down the stairs so fast he almost trips. We are hugging and kissing and crying. He pulls me up the stairs to his condo and opens the door.

"Guess who's here – the bum!"

Bercu's wife comes running out of the kitchen.

There is more hugging and kissing and crying.

A young man and woman are also in the apartment. The young man is twice my size and wearing an Israeli army uniform.

"You remember our son?"

I remember a baby, not this giant. We shake hands. He introduces his wife, I introduce Suzy, and we all sit down.

—

I wanted to take everyone out to a nice restaurant, but Bercu's wife insisted on cooking us a meal – and she was a great cook. We ate like horses and talked about old times. Bercu did most of the talking, speaking in Yiddish so Suzy would understand. He told her all about my life in Beregszasz; how sick my mother was, how my father's stepsister, Yolanka, moved into the house and looked after me.... "She was so good to him. We all spoiled him rotten."

Tears were running down Suzy's face as Bercu told his stories. He remembered everything in perfect detail, as if we had never been separated. But there was something different about Bercu. I couldn't figure out what it was. Then, as he continued to talk, it hit me: Bercu wasn't stuttering. He had lost his speech impediment.

I asked him about my father's other worker, Gabi, who was also living in Israel. He had been very kind to me when I returned from the camps, even offering to adopt me, and I wanted to look him up. Bercu discouraged me.

"Why bother him? He's an old man; he won't even recognize you."

I asked him about Duni.

"Don't worry, he's not running away. We'll go and see him together."

I wanted to see Duni alone, but I had no choice but to accept Bercu's offer. Bercu hadn't seen me in thirty-five years and now he wasn't going to let me out of his sight. So the next day we *both* went to see my boyhood friend.

Once again I didn't call ahead, and when Duni saw me at the door he almost passed out.

"I didn't know if you were dead or alive. Why didn't you write?"

What could I say?

I didn't have to say anything – Duni had already forgiven me.

"Yeah, I understand, we all get tied up in our own lives."

"What happened to you – did you go aliyah bet?"

"No, the madrichim decided that the younger guys should wait until we could emigrate legally."

After I left for Canada, Duni had stayed at the kinderhaim for another six months. Then the State of Israel was declared, and the gates were opened. The British were the first ones through, heading out. They didn't say goodbye, just packed up their equipment (or turned it over to the Arabs) and left the fledgling nation to the mercy of her neighbours. Arab armies attacked from three sides, vowing to drive the Jews into the sea. To avoid annihilation, tiny Israel recruited every able-bodied man, woman, and grown-up child. The Israeli Defense Force consisted of a handful of British-trained Sabras leading an army of Holocaust survivors. Duni was taken into the army as soon as he stepped off the boat. "They gave us two weeks basic training and sent us to the front," he said. "But the Arabs attacked our convoy and we were virtually wiped out." Tears came into his eyes. "Some of the remains of the trucks are still there. If you like, I'll show you the spot."

Next day Duni took me to see a string of bombed-out trucks sitting beside the road, marked by a memorial plaque: *This is where the children who survived the holocaust were killed*.

Duni brought out a stack of photographs from Italy – the ones I had taken when I had money in my pocket – and they stirred up pleasant memories. There was a picture of our soccer team: ten of us, dressed in our blue and white kibbutz uniforms. I was standing in the middle, the only one not smiling.

"What happened to the others?" I asked.

Duni pointed them out, one by one.

"This guy died, this guy died, this guy died …"

"A lot of the guys from the kibbutz died."

Duni nodded. "Forty-five out of a hundred." Even my nemesis, Silica, had been killed. "I don't know how we won," Duni said, shaking his head. Tears came into his eyes. "We were just kids; we didn't know anything about fighting a war. They gave us grenades to put in our belts. When some of the guys took them out, the grenades blew up before they could throw them. I was lucky – I just got a leg wound. After I got wounded, they made me a medic."

"A medic? You used to faint at the sight of blood!"

"I saw a *lot* of blood, Yakov."

Duni still had a young face, but his eyes had lost their sparkle.

"Our friends gave their lives defending this country and now the Israelis treat me like *I'm* the enemy." Duni worked as a policeman at the bus depot. It was a very stressful job. "It's not like at home – here, nobody listens to a policeman. If I give a cab driver a ticket, he's liable to attack me. The Sabras are the worst. It's their country and they'll park where they want!"

"I used to drive a cab," I said. "It's a tough way to make a living."

"If you think it's tough in Canada, you should try it here. If an Israeli cab driver has to pay a parking fine he can lose a day's income. I usually let them off with a warning. You want to see what I do for a living – come visit me at work tomorrow."

—

Duni had an office at the bus depot, a stuffy little cubbyhole. After watching him do paperwork for a while, I went outside for some fresh air.

Duni wasn't exaggerating – being a traffic cop here was a little more stressful than in Canada.

—

Duni and I spent a lot of time together in the following days. He took me to see his brother, Moshe,
who had also fought in the War of Liberation. Moshe
was very affectionate, hugging and kissing me. "This
is Duni's best friend," he said as he introduced me to
his wife, Marika.

Marika is a Hungarian name, so I said a few words
to her in that language.

She didn't understand.

"I'm from Romania," she said with a smile.

Moshe and Marika introduced me to their teenage
son, who became very excited when he heard we were
from Canada. In a few weeks he was going to visit a
friend in Toronto.

"Maybe I'll come to Winnipeg too."

"If you do, get in touch with me."

I gave him our address and phone number – but I
never heard from him.

Duni had an eighteen-year-old daughter who was
also dying to come to Canada. She wouldn't leave
us alone. Neither would Bercu, who expected me to
spend all my time with him. "Tomorrow," he would
say, whenever I asked to see Gabi. I was sorry Suzy
and I had gone on the tour the first week. Now we
had just six days to see dozens of people, and we were
being pulled from all sides. I knew my friends at home

would be mad at me for not visiting their relatives in Israel, but every night I would come home exhausted and fall asleep as soon as my head hit the pillow. The next thing I knew, we were back on the plane to Winnipeg. For the first time in two weeks, I had a chance to catch my breath.

Aftershock

Shortly after we returned from Israel, I went to see my doctor. By this time, Sam Peikoff was no longer practising so I was referred to Dr. Leonard Greenberg. While he was examining me, he asked questions about my trip to Israel. He referred me to a heart specialist because I had a heart problem (angina).

On October 15, 1984, I suffered a heart attack. My wife drove me to the St. Boniface Hospital emergency department, where I was examined by a resident doctor. He checked the EKG printout and didn't think I had had a heart attack. He told me to get dressed and go home. I try to sit up but I don't have the strength. I feel very sick. Another doctor by the name of Dr. Mymin walked by and asked, "What is the problem here?"

"I want to see his EKG. Where is his IV? Someone with chest pains should have an IV immediately!"

While the nurse is hooking me up, he checks the EKG and blows his top.

"Who is the doctor in charge?"

The nurse calls the resident on the intercom.

When he shows up, the doctor gives him hell.

He points to something on the EKG printout. "Didn't you see this? This man had a heart attack."

It was pure luck that one of the top cardiologists in the country happened to be walking down the hall as I was trying to get off that gurney. After the doctor finished bawling out his young colleague, he turned his attention to me and introduced himself.

"I'm Dr. Mymin."

—

Dr. Mymin sent me to the intensive care unit, where I spent the night. First thing next morning, he showed up with the results of my blood test.

"You have some heart damage, but it's not too bad. I'll keep you off your feet for a few days and if all goes well, you should be able to go home in two weeks."

—

For the first week, I stayed flat on my back Dr. Mymin wouldn't even let me get out of bed to go to the bathroom. Then after one more week in bed he prescribed medication and let me go home. After I recuperated, the City of Winnipeg gave me an option of light duty work. For a while, I was checking buses, and then I worked at city-owned golf courses. I did that for five years. Then I was put on total disability pension. In 1995, at age sixty-five, I retired from the transit system with gifts and good wishes.

Golden Years

My working days were over. The transit company gave me a disability pension after my heart attack. I spent the first few weeks of my retirement at home, recuperating. Friends came to visit and talked about old times to cheer me up. Old times in Winnipeg, that is. Whenever I talked to someone from my European past, I was upset for weeks. Yet I kept seeking these people out, hungry for any scrap of information they could give me. It was like a bad tooth that you keep poking with your tongue, even though you know it's painful. Not a day went by that I didn't think of my sister, Szidi, and wonder what had become of her.

Now that I was a man of leisure, Suzy and I began to spend part of the winter in "the Sun Belt." After my wife retired, we bought a place in Florida, but our first few trips were to Palm Springs, California, a two-hour drive from Los Angeles. One of my Mihaly cousins was living in L. A. so, on our first trip, my wife and I went to visit him. He greeted us cordially, served us coffee, and we talked for hours. But on the drive back to Palm Springs, Suzy asked me a strange question.

"Was your sister adopted by Gentiles, Jack?"

"No, by a Jewish couple. Why?"

"Your cousin told me she was adopted by Gentiles."

This was a shock to me and as far as I knew, it wasn't true. If Szidi had been adopted by Gentiles, there was a chance that she was still alive.

My cousin had planted a seed of doubt. Could he be right? Surely a person wouldn't make up a story like that. I couldn't stop thinking about it. Finally, back in Winnipeg, I decided to get in touch with another cousin whom I hadn't spoken to in years: Shmule Doovid Blau, who lived in New York, had a memory like a computer.

I telephoned him. After we made some small talk, I got to the point.

"Is it true my sister Szidi was adopted by Gentiles?"

"Don't be crazy. Who told you that, Mihaly?"

"Yes."

"He's a Goy himself."

I felt like I was twelve years old again. My cousins were still carrying on the old family feud. I had tried to move on with my life, but for them time stood still. It was as if they had never left the old country. The Nazis had butchered the parents, and the children had survived by a miracle, but it hadn't affected their outlook at all – they were as small-minded and spiteful as ever.

"Before the Germans arrived," Shmule Doovid went on, "your sister's new father came to see me – he wanted to know if I had any papers for her – and he was a Jew. Your sister was brought up in a good Jewish home, Weisz. You should have been so lucky. We offered to take you, you know."

"I know."

"Well, it's too late now. Does your wife at least observe the dietary laws?"

"Yes, she keeps a kosher house."

"No children?"

"We have two boys."

"Did they have Bar Mitzvahs?"

"A long time ago – they're both married."

"To Jewish girls?"

"Lovely Jewish girls."

"Do you go to schule (synagogue)?"

"We buy seats for the High Holidays every year. When my kids were young, they went on Saturday morning too."

"Never mind the kids, what about the father?"

"Most Saturdays I had to drive a bus."

"You worked on Shabbas (Sabbath)?"

"This isn't Israel; buses run on Shabbas too."

"You're a Goy," Shmule Doovid said.

It was a familiar refrain. Anyone who didn't live up to Shmule Doovid's fanatically Orthodox standards was a Gentile. Ordinarily I would have hung up on him, but what he told me about Szidi had lifted such a load from my mind that I was prepared to ignore the remark. We talked for another forty-five minutes. But just before I hung up, I got even with him.

"I haven't seen you in such a long time, Shmule Doovid, that I probably wouldn't recognize you. By now you must have a long beard."

"I don't have a beard. I work for a wholesale grocer and they don't allow it."

"You shave?"

"I have no choice, it's a health regulation."

"So you're a Goy too," I said and hung up.

—

After speaking to Shmule Doovid, I felt relieved, but it wasn't long before the doubts started creeping back in. What if my cousin had made up his story just to spite Mihaly? A few years later, when Suzy and I were in California again, I decided to confront Mihaly with the story Blau had told me.

I telephoned from Palm Springs and his wife, Magda, answered the phone.

She told me she was now a widow.

"He died almost a year ago. The unveiling is tomorrow."

Sue and I drove into Los Angeles for the unveiling, where we met my cousin's son and daughter-in-law. After the unveiling, we went back to the house for refreshments. I took Magda aside and asked if her husband had ever mentioned my sister.

She could not recall.

"But it's funny you asked – there's a man from Fekete Ardo who's visiting his daughter in L. A. Maybe you should talk to him."

Fehkete Ardo was the town where Szidi had lived with her adoptive parents. Sue and I drove straight to the house in L. A., even thought it was already nine o'clock at night.

The man's daughter answered the door.

Her father wasn't home, but she expected him back in an hour.

"Do you mind if we wait?"

"Of course not. Come in."

We waited until eleven, but the man didn't show up and we couldn't wait any longer.

"We have to drive back to Palm Springs. I'll call your father tomorrow – I'd like him to make some inquiries for me when he gets back to Fehkete Ardo."

I gave her some money to cover his expenses.

The next day I phoned and spoke to her father, who was very obliging.

"Of course I don't mind – I live right there. Don't worry, I'll find out for you."

Several months passed and I didn't hear anything. I was disappointed but not really surprised. Why should this man put himself out for a stranger? He had probably made a few inquiries, got nowhere, and forgotten about it. So I tried to forget about it too.

Then one day I received a letter with a Soviet postmark. I opened the envelope with shaky hands and took out the contents – several handwritten pages and an old photograph of my sister and her adoptive parents. I looked at the photographs and felt tightness in my chest. As I started to read the letter, which was written in Hungarian, my heart was pounding:

June 26th, 1991

Dear Sir:

First of all I would like to apologize for taking so long to get back to you. I didn't have the information until now, so I couldn't get back to you sooner. The little information you had about your sister led me to a lot of dead ends and I had to start all over again. It was like looking for a needle in a haystack. The older people hardly remember what happened so many years ago, and many of them didn't want to talk about it. There was a point when I felt I had to give up the search but my perseverance and belief that I would succeed paid off. I have the correct information for you now, although it is very tragic and painful. I finally met a woman who was a very close friend of Hanna Elias, you sister's adoptive mother. She gave me a picture of the three of them together, Deza and Hanna Elias and Szidi. This is what she told me. Szidi's adoptive parents were very caring and loving people. She was their only child and was very precious to them. Then the tragedy happened – the deportation.

Deza Elias was in the army and then sent to a labour camp. Hanna Elias didn't want to be separated from Szidi so they were both taken to the ghetto in Nagyszolos. The friend accompanied Hanna and Szidi to a point where

she was allowed to go – a small town called Szaszfalu,
not far from Nagyszolos. Szidi and Hanna didn't stay in
the ghetto long; they were shipped to Auschwitz. After the
war they never came back. Deza Elias was in a labour
camp. They never took him to Auschwitz. In 1945 after
the war some people saw him in Halmi, Romania, and
he was making inquiries as to what happened to his wife
and daughter. They told him they never came back. They
probably got sick and died or were put to death in the gas
chamber. He had no reason to go home and he was going
to leave the country.

I am sorry to give you this sad news. I have nothing
more to report. If by chance I will find out anything else I
will let you know. If you get any more information let me
know and I will see what I can find out.

Borchik Miklos
U.S.S.R. – 295536
Zakarpatskaja, obl.
Vinogradovski r-n

I read the letter five times. I've never stopped looking
at the picture. It's the only one I have of my beautiful
sister.

SUMMING UP

Well, that's the story of my life – so far. It's been more than twenty years since I had my heart attack and I'm still around to play golf with my friends and drive my grandchildren to the Dark Zone to play video games on their friends' birthdays. In the summer of 2000, the whole family went to Israel to celebrate three of my grandchildren's Bar/Bat Mitzvahs. Suzy has retired and we spend part of the winter in Florida and most of the summer at our cottage on Lake Winnipeg. The life I'm living today is beyond my wildest childhood dreams.

As a child, my wildest dream was to wake up in a dry bed. In the camps, I didn't dream at all – just waking up in the morning was an achievement. Finding a few soggy vegetables in my can of hot-water soup at the end of the day was my wildest dream. When it takes all your mental and physical energy just to survive from day to day, dreaming is an extravagance you can't afford.

Why did I survive when so many others perished? I don't know. If not for a series of seemingly unrelated and unexplainable events, I would have perished a

Friends, Israel, 2000.

dozen times. If I hadn't refused to carry my stepmother's bundle; if a couple of complete strangers hadn't
noticed my Hungarian scout cap; if a German soldier
hadn't got tired of chasing me; if a couple of half-dead

Our family, Israel, 2000.

Heftlings hadn't carried me on the death march ... it defies rational explanation. I can understand why three starving Heftlings would steal my bread but not why two others would use their last remaining strength to save my life. The only explanation is that a guard put a gun to their heads. But why would a Nazi guard single out one Jew for such mercy when others were being killed like flies? I think God must have had something to do with it – God and my mother.

Whenever I think about that "miracle," I remember how my mother took me into her deathbed when I was three years old. "What's going to happen when I die?" she had asked. Orthodox Jews believe that when a good person dies, she can watch over her loved ones from the other world.

I'm not an Orthodox Jew, but I believe my mother has been watching over me.

—

As I said at the very beginning, I have a problem – a problem that I'm sure afflicts many other survivors as well. I suffer from constant nightmares, which affects my life.

"If you wrote about it," my wife suggested to me once, "maybe the nightmares would stop. Or, at least, not be so bad. If you don't want to do it for yourself, do it for the kids. So they'll know what happened to you."

The idea didn't appeal to me. "You want me to sit down and write a book? I don't have the patience to *read* a book."

"You don't have to write it down; you can tell it to me. I'll type it up. It will give you something to do."

It would also give *her* something to do. Suzy had been working since she was a young girl and now she had nothing but time on her hands.

My wife had worked for years as executive secretary of the Talmud Torah and Joseph Wolinsky Collegiate, but working as her husband's secretary for a few months was a tougher job. She had to pull the words out of me – and they didn't come out in a straight line.

I thought we would never finish. But finally we did. The story of my life took just over thirty pages to tell. Suzy put a cover on it and we gave it to our sons to read. They were very moved.

I met with my collaborator on this book a number of times over the next few months, and we taped hours of interviews. Sometimes I would refresh my memory by talking to a fellow survivor. We had never discussed these things – for fifty years we had kept them inside. Then in 1998 – the fiftieth anniversary of our arrival in Canada – we survivors suddenly became celebrities. My friends and I were interviewed by newspaper reporters and on television. The Holocaust, a forbidden subject for half a century, became a media event. A crew from Steven Spielberg's Shoah Project arrived at my house to videotape my story for posterity. Rebecca (Lyons) Bergman, our chaperone on the train to Winnipeg fifty years earlier, came in from Israel and we had a pleasant reunion. It was an eye-opening experience. I heard things about my best friends that I had never heard before. One of them broke down in front of the camera. He had lost his whole family. Everyone had a different story. We came from the same place but were completely different people.

"Do you have nightmares?" I asked one of my survivor friends.

"Never," he said. "I sleep like a baby."

He wanted me to describe my nightmares, but I couldn't remember the details – just that they were usually about the death march. "Try writing them down," he suggested, but I couldn't do it. When you wake up in the middle of the night with your heart pounding, having just escaped from a bad dream, the last thing you want to do is revisit that nightmare world. Still, as I continued to go over the story of my life with my collaborator, the nightmares seemed to be less frequent. The night before our last meeting, I had a dream that was completely different – one that was so vivid I was able to remember every detail without writing it down:

I'm living on a kibbutz in Israel. My cousins and children are living there too. I'm sitting on a porch in a rocking chair with my youngest granddaughters, Lauren and Marly, on my lap. Marly is sucking her thumb.

One of my cousins walks up and says, "Herman's back in town."

Herman is the cousin who suggested we go back to Beregszasz to look for my sister.

I jump up and head for his house, carrying my grandchildren.

"You're going to see my sister," I tell them. "Your great auntie."

We arrive at Herman's house. I go up the steps and open the door. I see Herman and two nice-looking young women in their mid-twenties. They are playing and laughing.

When I come in, they run into another room – they're shy around strangers.

"Herman, did you find my sister?"

He smiles.

"Do you know who those girls are?"

I shake my head.

"Szidi's daughters."

I feel a surge of happiness. I go into the room to see the girls. I try to put my grandchildren down, but they don't want to go, so I hold them in one arm and hug my nieces with the other. It's such a good feeling.

"Where is your mother?"

Herman answers from behind me.

"Szidi's safe. She doesn't want to come yet."

I turn around.

"But I want to see her."

"You can go and visit her anytime," Herman says. "She's at home."

And then I woke up – feeling wonderful.